ENDORSEMENTS

It is difficult to overstate the importance of Dr Penny Burns with regard to Public Infrastructure in Australia. Prior to her work in the Engineering and Water Supply (E&WS) Department in South Australia, there had been the general assumption that assets could be acquired and that the maintenance of those assets could be left to future governments to address on a 'needs' basis — a typical cash accounting attitude that was only just giving way to the need for accrual accounting.

Penny successfully challenged that assumption and her subsequent work for the South Australian Parliamentary Public Accounts Committee enabled a wide dissemination of both her views and the methodology she used to provide a 'whole of life' cost of an asset.

She was so successful that when portfolios were being redistributed in 1992, I found myself appointed Minister of Public Infrastructure, the first such appointment in South Australian history. By a quirk of fate, the portfolio included the E&WS.

Penny had moved to Tasmania by this time and was rapidly becoming the person to go to for asset management matters on both the national and international scene.

Her book provides a fascinating insight into how a single person can influence the way we look at an existing concept through the lens of a different perspective; as well as providing a history of how such a new perspective can be developed.

John Klunder
Former Chairman, Public Accounts Committee of South Australia
Former Minister, South Australia

Dr. Penny Burns' wit and wisdom shine through with absorbing tales of her exploits in pioneering asset management. Part memoir, part manifesto, she entertains and enlightens readers with the inside story behind quantifying the true costs of public infrastructure, revealing the massive unseen burden facing people in the future. Tracing her journey challenging established methods and mindsets, Penny makes a compelling case for revolutionizing infrastructure planning with new ways of thinking. Her infectious enthusiasm for ideas makes this call to action a must-read.

Lou Cripps
Regional Transportation District, Denver, Colorado
Co-author of *Building an Asset Management Team*

The Story of Asset Management reminds us that we are all making trade-offs between what is urgent today versus what is important for tomorrow. Penny's personal story, entwined with years of curiosity, challenging norms, and seeking better, is shared in a simple yet profoundly powerful way. We are all asset managers at heart and Penny's term 'historical moral responsibility' empowers us to shape the future.

Martin Kerr
Director, Structured Change, Sydney, NSW
Co-author, *Living Asset Management Maturity*

Are you interested in delivering valuable public services? Do you manage infrastructure? Is the world changing around you? Dr Burns' book tells the story of how the need for asset management was identified, formed, and incorporated into the inner workings of governments throughout Australia. It's readable, deeply informative, and very useful to those of us facing challenges in delivering valuable public services. Highly recommended.

Kerry McGovern, Brisbane, Queensland
Founder, EAROPH Australia
Co-author, *Infrastructure Maintenance in the Pacific: challenging the*
build-neglect-rebuild paradigm

Asset management is proving hard to get hold of. It isn't 'maintenance plus' or a new type of engineering. It isn't organisational design. It isn't digital analytics. It isn't business strategy. It isn't an efficiency program. It isn't a management standard. It's all of these and more — a powerful far-reaching logic to be applied wherever the success of a business or the quality of a service is dependent on physical or knowledge assets.

This book is a reminder that it is people — with all their personal motivations, career agendas, political ambitions, passions, and fads — who lie at the heart of getting the relationships between money, risk, and performance right for shareholders, investors, taxpayers, communities, and the planet.

Asset management professionals should step back from the hubbub, find a quiet space, read it, and reflect on what they are doing and whether it is good enough.

Chris Lloyd, CAS, UK
Co-Editor, *Asset Management: transforming asset dependent businesses*

The Story of Asset Management by Dr. Penny Burns is a milestone work on the history of asset management. Financing, maintaining, and replacing our physical infrastructure are crucial to our future. With 35 years of experience in public sector asset management at the United States Government Accountability Office and the New York City Office of Management and Budget, I can truly say that Penny is a trailblazer for women in the field. I would compare her to Billie Jean King for tennis.

Amelia Shachoy, MPA, PMP
Federal Audit Office AM team, USA

Penny Burns is, along with being a great writer: bold, persistent, curious, unafraid of new ideas and still looking for them as she sails on in her 9th decade. So smart she would make the rest of us feel dim, except that she is boundless in her enthusiasm for sharing ideas and knowledge. Clarity in a very, very muddled world.

Ruth Wallsgrove, AMCL
Co-author, *Building an Asset Management Team*

In the beginning, Penny led engineers to consider refurbishment and replacement costs, from which she developed, with the Public Accounts Committee, the model used today for forecasting asset renewal. Her interests and network expanded to finance, government treasury, and politicians; and then to accounting, audit, and legislation.

Penny thinks and works simultaneously in the short and long term, and her thinking is both global and analytical. Fortunately, she has an easy writing style that makes the story come alive, with many anecdotes that experienced asset managers will relate to, and newer asset managers will enjoy — and hopefully be encouraged by seeing how major changes were made in quite simple steps.

Every professional needs to know the origins of their profession.

Bob Ritchie
Former Secretary to the Public Accounts Committee, South Australia
Author, *Practitioner's Guide to Experiential Learning*

INFRASTRUCTURE

we can afford
TO BUY IT.

can we afford
TO KEEP IT?

The Story of
Asset Management

DR PENNY BURNS

Published in 2023 by Dr Penny Burns
Adelaide, Australia
www.talkinginfrastructure.com

Author: Dr Penny Burns
Title: The Story of Asset Management
Print ISBN: 9780645941425
Ebook ISBN: 9780645941418
Subjects: Infrastructure, Economics, Asset Management

Registered with the National Library of Australia
Book production services: www.smartwomenpublish.com

Disclaimer:
The material in this publication is of the nature of general comment only and does not represent professional advice. All material is provided for educational purposes only. We recommend to always seek the advice of a qualified professional before making any decision regarding personal and business needs. To the maximum extent permitted by law, the author and publisher disclaim all responsibility and liability to any person arising directly or indirectly from any person taking or not taking action based on the information in this publication.

DEDICATED TO

My father, who inspired me to aim high, and my mother, my brother Ron, and my husband Bob, who were always there for me when I bit off a bit too much.

And to my daughters, Mercedes and Sheridan, and their families — indeed, all families, now and future, who provide the motivation to continually strive for better asset management.

ACKNOWLEDGEMENTS

I once observed that I had never met an Asset Manager I didn't like. How could you not like imaginative, innovative people who are prepared to challenge the status quo for the sake of the community at large, for the welfare of people they have never met? In future volumes, we will meet many of them.

Some, however, deserve special mention here for being some of the earliest to move out into the unknown. Firstly, Alan Herath, Manager of Corporate Planning at the Engineering and Water Supply Department, took a chance on me and allowed me to follow up on the first question that started the chain of all to follow. Then, Bob Ritchie, Secretary of the Parliamentary Public Accounts Committee, recognised the value of what had been learnt about water assets and saw advantage in knowing this for all state infrastructure. He convinced the committee to break with its traditional studies in order to follow it up, then worked with me to produce our eight reports. These reports, however, might have languished unaddressed had Bob not provided the insight that enabled me to continue with my work in asset m anagement after my work with the committee finished.

The quality of those reports, and thus their acceptance, is also due to John Klunder, the Chair of the Public Accounts Committee, who provided superb chairmanship and consistent support for the project. Dean Lambert, at the Department of Construction, both supported and challenged, and both actions are gratefully acknowledged. And, of course, Michael Weldon, the Minister for Construction, Resources and Energy in Tasmania, must be thanked for going out on a limb to give me the most wonderful opportunity to expand my thinking beyond a single agency.

Then there are those rare thinkers whose early conversations set off a whole stream of ideas; people like Ted Smithies and Alan Butler of the Value Management team at NSW Public Works, whom I met early in my explorations after the PAC (and my apologies to the staff in the adjoining office for the level of laughter that inevitably accompanied our discussions). Also with NSW Public Works was Jeff Powys, whose rare ability to foresee future issues so very accurately changed the direction of my thoughts many times.

I would particularly like to thank Chris Adam, of StrategicAM in Queensland, with whom I have had numerous conversations over the years and learnt so much. His contribution to Part 4, about the difficulty of applying marginal cost to infrastructure where the objectives are much wider than mere dollars, is particularly appreciated. I am also more than grateful to Kerry McGovern of K. McGovern and Associates, Queensland, for her wide knowledge of the area, and for her auditor's attention to detail in reviewing the entire text, which has greatly improved it.

This volume, of course, would not have seen the light of day had it not been for the constant support, involvement, and encouragement of the diverse and talented Talking Infrastructure Board. We have:

CEO Jeff Roorda, Engineer, and Director of Economy, Place and Infrastructure at the Blue Mountains City Council, NSW, an area of rare beauty, heritage and tourism, which is at constant risk of environmental damage, placing extra responsibility on sound infrastructure decision making and asset management.

Ruth Wallsgrove, Historian and Writer, Fellow of the Institute of Asset Management, and gifted communicator who is the Lead Asset Management Trainer for AMCL, North America. Based in London, she has trained thousands of asset managers on five continents. She is my co-writer for the Talking Infrastructure Blog, and her skills include being a master practitioner of NLP.

Gregory Punshon, Engineer at Consulto, NSW, and the Board's Strategic Technology Advisor. At the Gosford City Council, he was instrumental in securing the first carrier licence for local government to operate a telco network and infrastructure. I first met Gregory after a serious accident had occurred in Gosford, and his work in asset management and his communication skills were able to completely turn around extremely negative media reporting.

Lou Cripps, Business/Commerce. Lou is Director of Asset Management, at the Regional Transportation District, Denver, Colorado. His skills and training in team leadership are demonstrated in his book *Building an Asset Management Team,* which he co-authored with Ruth Wallsgrove for Talking Infrastructure. Lou is invaluable as the board's 'man on the front line', keeping us up to date with the daily challenges of an asset management team leader in an area that is both politically sensitive and subject to constant change.

Over the last 40 years, I have worked with and exchanged ideas with a great many talented asset managers and can happily attest that asset management has gathered a great tribe to belong to!

HOW THE STORY UNFOLDS

Here we consider how seeing asset management as the unravelling of a fascinating problem over time, and with the involvement of many, makes this story possible.

In April 1994, as the first economist in the then 110-year history of the South Australian state water authority, a comment by the Minister of Water generated my first question.

The minister had said we would charge irrigators what it cost to supply them with water, but we did not know these costs or any of our infrastructure costs. In this chapter, we look at how we found the answer to our first question:

Question 1: What is it costing South Australians to get their water services?

Once we had determined current costs, we set out to forecast asset renewal in order to answer the next logical question:

Question 2: What will it cost to replace aging water assets and when will this likely occur?

The answer to question 2 showed that our renewal costs were set to rise sharply — but this would not happen just yet; we had time to plan. However, other infrastructure agencies would likely also have rising costs and we didn't know what they would be.

Word of what we were doing had spread and the Parliamentary Public Accounts Committee was interested to know what the situation would be like for other infrastructure agencies. I was asked to find out.

In February 1985, with the South Australian Parliamentary Public Accounts Committee, I applied the asset renewal prototype to the major infrastructure users in the state: public housing, hospitals, highways, transport, schools and colleges, power and water, or 80% of the state's infrastructure.

Here public housing renewal is presented as a case study, with examples also drawn from the other agencies, in order to answer:

Question 3: What is the future cost to the state of all major infrastructure renewal?

The cost projections made it clear that we could not afford to continue 'as is'. This is what the committee recommended should be done to answer:

Question 4: How can we contain these renewal costs?

Here we consider the reactions of the parliament itself, the government, media, and others. Interest was extensive.

My next move was to public works which presented an opportunity to implement the recommendations made by the committee.

In April 1987, with the Department of Housing and Construction (South Australian public works), the challenge was to create interest in implementing solutions to the asset management problem.

Stumbling the way to success can lead to useful discoveries. A task focus is fine, but an understanding of people is essential in order to answer:

Question 5: How can the PAC recommendations be implemented?

For attitudes to change, those making the change must see the benefits. How could future and potential benefits be made visible in the present? This was essential to tackle:

Question 6: How do we appeal to architecture, audit, and other disciplines?

As we spread the results of the renewal study, we gathered more reactions, now from practitioners, policy makers and, importantly, from the large infrastructure developers.

One particular conference presentation was responsible for the opportunity to extend the possibilities of asset management beyond improving agency performance.

In August 1989, I was offered the role as Advisor to the Minister of Construction, Resources and Energy in Tasmania. This was a time of much administrative change in Australia, and also a time of severe financial distress for Tasmania. Could asset management help the state?

By 1989 many changes were taking place — in accounting, finance, regulation, and administration, as well as asset management. Asset management was no longer the 'only game in town' and we needed to consider:

Question 7: What are the new AM considerations to be borne in mind when everything is changing?

What can the 'important' issue of asset management offer at a time when the 'urgent' issue of finance and cost reduction is dominant? This was necessary to answer:

Question 8: How can asset management help in situations of severe financial distress?

In this time of change, much could be learnt from the reactions of those involved.

This next change was my last: I stopped being an employee and became an advisor in asset management strategy.

From March 1992, I had much greater freedom to move around the country and be engaged in the work of many individual and central agencies as they sought to encompass asset management.

I now had enough knowledge of different aspects of, and uses for, asset management to tackle a critical question for integrating asset management into the general practice or 'the way we do things around here'. Here is how I approached the next question:

Question 9: How can the benefits of asset management be best conveyed to those who do not yet know?

Until now all my questions were those I asked myself. But this was asked of me when I began to consider writing this story, and it is a good way to finish this volume:

Question 10: What kind of a story are you intending to tell?

Some asset managers deal with assets in agencies where there is a clear 'bottom line' that can be employed to justify action. Others are not so fortunate. In each case, circumstances shape the way they see the issues of asset management. Here we consider some of the differences.

The next volume is designed to capture the experience of many practiced asset managers, so as a preview, here we share stories told by three leading pioneers in the field — and by one young and very enthusiastic recruit whose story, I think, sums up everything that is exciting about asset management.

PREFACE

My father was a master storyteller, and when I was about seven or eight he would tell me stories in which the main character was me — but grown-up. My character would nightly solve many impossible problems using logic and courage. That fictional self was inspirational, and I grew up believing I was a problem solver ... so naturally, I looked for problems to solve.

In 1976, when I came to do my PhD, I had become intrigued with the idea of experimenting in economics. At that time, it was generally held to be impossible. In fact, economics lecturers would tell their first-year students in their very first lecture that this was why economics was so difficult. But was this true? Was it really impossible to experiment in economics? A nice problem.

I decided to use my PhD to find out whether experimentation was possible, and if so, was it able to do anything that other economic techniques could not? The answer to both questions turned out to be yes. However, this was an entirely new field. There were no guidelines as to what was needed and, in the event, I clearly overdid it. I designed, conducted, and analysed four separate studies, involving several hundred experiments, and then set them within an analytical framework. Instead of two years, it took me over five, only to find that just one of the individual studies would have been sufficient for a PhD. Such is the problem of working in the unknown.

However, while the extra work may not have been necessary for my thesis, it served a valuable purpose in generating support for the new idea of experimentation in economics. My fellow lecturers and tutors, and hundreds of the students, had taken part in the experiments, and many of the staff had helped me conduct them. They had lived through five years of this work and had seen it develop. They felt connected to it. They became enthusiasts and joined me in celebrating eventual success. We then worked together to create a research foundation to further the work. Much has happened since then, and today, what was once considered impossible is now a sub-discipline of economics in its own right, and the University of Adelaide has its own experimental economics laboratory. I doubt this would have happened if I had done the bare minimum.

This experience taught me three things:

- Just because something hasn't been done, doesn't mean it can't be;
- Much can be accomplished — 'with a little help from our friends'; and
- Anything worthwhile is worth putting considerable time and effort into.

These things would also prove to be true when, a few years later, I started to work on what would become asset management. This was an even more interesting problem, one that would occupy me not for just five years, but for the rest of my life. It would also introduce me to a great many people, in both practice and policy, who were equally interested in seeing the field develop.

Because I always saw asset management as an interesting problem to be unravelled, not simply as an outcome to be achieved, I was fascinated with the process from the beginning. Had it been just a private interest project, there would be little to talk about today. Asset management grew because many came to think of it as worthwhile.

This book is the story of that process. It follows a logical series of ten questions that arose between 1984 and 1993. During that time, I held five different positions, each of which suggested the questions and provided the opportunity to answer them — or, at the very least, to give it a good try.

This story is thus told in five parts, one for each role. Each of the first two chapters in each part covers one of the questions that I tackled in that role, how the question arose, and how it was addressed. In textbooks, an action is implemented and the solution just arrives, but in real life, it is not so simple. People react, some positively, some negatively, many mystified, and it all provides important information for progress. Thus, the third chapter in each part of our story looks at reactions.

My experience with asset management was unique in that I was able to consistently follow it over these different roles and places for ten years, developing and adding to a policy framework until it had gathered a sufficient quantum of support to continue under its own steam. Just how this happened is recounted in the fourth chapter of each part, called 'Moving On - My Story'.

For 30 years, I was actively involved in developing asset management strategy. Today I am an observer and chronicler. New opportunities to make progress are still arising, which you will discover when you follow the activities on our website, Talking Infrastructure. There you can find and download the articles referred to in this story, as well as information on our next venture, where we look at 'what worked in asset management, what didn't, and why', providing an opportunity for all asset managers to share their experiences.

All this at www.talkinginfrastructure.com/tams.

PART ONE: CURIOSITY

NOVEMBER 1982 - FEBRUARY 1985

THE ENGINEERING AND WATER SUPPLY DEPARTMENT

The first part of this story covers my time with the South Australian Engineering and Water Supply Department (the EWS), where I was the first economist in the 110-year history of the organisation. Some 15 months in, I came upon the question that set off the chain of questions that led to the development of asset management.

CHAPTER 1

HOW IT STARTED

In 1984, almost all infrastructure services in South Australia were provided by the state government, either through statutory authorities or budget-dependent departments. Where prices were set, as for water and sewerage, they were determined politically or to achieve a given policy. They were not based on costs. They couldn't be. We didn't know them (although we thought we did). This was as true of water as of other services. So it was that asset management started with a simple question to the EWS:

Q 1: WHAT IS IT COSTING SOUTH AUSTRALIANS TO GET THEIR WATER SERVICES?

This is how it happened.

It was April 1984, and we were listening to an announcement by Don Hopgood, the Minister for Water in South Australia, who had just declared that he was going to charge irrigators what it cost to supply water to them. Instinctively, I said, 'He can't do that!'

'Of course he can,' my corporate planning colleagues replied. 'He's the minister. He can do anything he likes.'

'I didn't say he wasn't *allowed to*. I said he *can't*. He doesn't have the information. *We* don't have it to give him. We don't have any capital costs, and even our recurrent costs are dicey.'

At that stage, I had been with the EWS, South Australia's water authority, which was responsible for the entire state, for about fifteen months. For that time, I had been working mostly on irrigation issues such as river salinity, water allocations, and transfers.

It suddenly struck me that I hadn't worked much on costs or prices which, given that I am an economist, might seem rather strange. However, it hadn't been necessary: water prices were set politically or to achieve policy ends. They had never, at least until this announcement, been based on costs.

Signs of things to come

What I didn't know then was that this decision by the Minister for Water was a harbinger of widespread changes across the public service over the next ten years. The full costs of infrastructure were beginning to be identified as the post-war boom in building infrastructure transitioned to the management of that infrastructure. Continued expansion wasn't sustainable — we didn't have the money.

Prime Minister Margaret Thatcher in the UK and President Ronald Reagan in the USA had restructured their economies in ways inspired by Milton Friedman's monetary theory. In doing so, they looked to transfer costs onto users and other beneficiaries rather than taxpayers. This was now affecting Australian policy.

It is impossible to understand the development of asset management in the absence of an understanding of this pivot point in economic policy. The private sector felt it could no longer expand its market share through innovation. Instead, it began looking to expand into the well-funded public sector. Its advocates, arguing that private sector entities were better managers, called for government trading enterprises to be transformed into self-funding corporate bodies. This then presented an opportunity for private sector entities to acquire public assets that were seriously undervalued. When privatisation followed corporatisation, the private sector gained a secure foothold in what had previously been public sector roles and responsibilities.

Efficiency now trumped effectiveness, with the objective of minimising costs easily dominating service outcomes. Return on investment was now applied to infrastructure, and only economic or financial returns were counted; social and environmental benefits were not factored in.

In the wake of the COVID-19 pandemic (2020–2022), we are beginning to rethink this approach, and many others that developed after the privatisation shift. We are now looking to resilience rather than the minimum cost to one entity, which externalises significant social and environmental costs. This shift will probably require fundamental changes to our infrastructure decision-making processes and a new set of fruitful questions that will lead to real improvement, not just change. So here, in preparation, I want to look back at the changes we have experienced already and the questions that inspired these changes more than thirty years ago.

How much does it cost?

When it is so common in history for innovative ideas to be sparked by unexpected events and opportunities, why is it that 'taking advantage of opportunities' has developed such a negative connotation? The asset management story is very much about the positive community benefits that arise from well-intentioned people taking advantage of opportunities.

The announcement by the Minister for Water is a case in point. After we had examined why it was that we did not have the information the minister would need to charge 'what it costs to supply water to irrigators' (principally because we lacked information on our capital holdings), we realised that this equally applied to all the services we provided — water and sewer provision, as well as such research activities as investigating rainfall in the arid north of the state.

So that afternoon, I asked Alan Herath, our corporate policy branch manager, whether he would like to know how much it was costing South Australians to get their water and sewer services — not what we were charging them, but what it was really costing.

His eyes lit up, and he said he would very much like to know that. I wasn't surprised; Alan was a very forward-thinking engineer. After all, it was he who had decided that the department needed an economist and had appointed me to the position as the first EWS economist in the 110 years of its operations.

However, at this stage, I started to have a twinge of doubt. I didn't know how the other branches and divisions might interpret such an inquiry by corporate planning. Fifteen months on the job had given me some insight into internal politics, but not yet enough to be sure of working my way through them. So, I tentatively suggested he might like to think about it overnight. He did, and was still of the same opinion the following morning.

The game was afoot

Or was it? I now had to figure out what our capital costs were. A little bit of exposure to the accounting system by this time had shown that our records were still handwritten on file cards (this was 1984). Moreover, on these cards, an expenditure of $500 in 1984 was considered to represent the same amount of acquisition as it would have in 1964 or 1944, regardless of the changing dollar values. No distinction was made between capital acquisitions that replaced something that had worn out or failed and those that expanded the stock. When an asset failed and was withdrawn from service, its value was not removed from these financial records.

This made the financial records extremely suspect, and I was reluctant to use them or even to approach the finance section for assistance, for I imagined that if I did, I would be taken by the hand down into the basement and shown decades of dusty file cards with the instruction (along with a wry grin) to 'help myself'. Later, I realised that these records only covered what the department had spent out of its own funds and did not include the very large federal grants that were made in the early years, or the (also large) developer-funded assets we acquired as our suburbs expanded in the later years. I needed to find another way.

What had I let myself in for? As an economist, it was natural to start by thinking about the numbers — the financial data — and I did. But everything I thought of came up against the problems listed above. It wasn't until I had exhausted all possible financial data approaches and switched to focusing on what we were really talking about — namely, the physical infrastructure — that I had a working alternative.

So, one afternoon I sat down with our internal auditor and asked, 'What different types of assets do we have?'

In one session, this brilliant fellow sketched on his whiteboard all the different classes of assets, from pipes and sewers to treatment stations to pumps and dams. What's more, he gave me the name of the guy in charge of each asset, who would know most about it. In only two cases was it necessary for me to be passed on to another person, so his knowledge was excellent.

Data collection

Then I had to start my own data collection. Here my difficulty was the engineer's natural tendency to dive into detail. Economists, as everyone knows, are happy with approximations and assumptions. Not so engineers, for obvious and sound reasons.

So, I did what Paul Van der Lee, my section leader, had done for me when I started working in the EWS. Knowing that I had spent the previous fifteen years in academia, where perfection rather than timeliness was of the essence, he would say to me, 'Penny, this is a half-day exercise' or 'Just one page will do, and I need it by Friday.' I much appreciated that. So I applied it to this job. I would generally say something like, 'This is a half-day exercise. If you think it will take more, stop. Call me.'

In 1984, we had yet to experience the mass downsizing of the public service and the loss of experienced engineers that was to come about five years later. The senior engineers I spoke with had many years of experience in the department and knew their assets very well indeed.

I talked at length with each of them, and we looked at what assets they had, how old they were, and when they might need to be renewed or repaired. We spoke of the history of the assets, the peak construction periods, the impact of World War II and its limitations on materials and qualified personnel, and other changes experienced since then, such as the increasing involvement of developers in the choice, design and construction of assets that they then handed over to the department to manage. Fortuitously, the department had just finished a commissioned engineering study of all its underground pipes and sewers, so a condition assessment of these assets was to hand.

That meant that, in just three weeks, I had spoken with each technical expert and had gotten a clear idea of exactly what assets we had, their condition, how long they typically lasted, and how old they were. So that was size, age, economic life, and residual life accounted for.

Incidentally, after I left the EWS for the Public Accounts Committee (PAC), a team of seven engineers spent about eighteen months reviewing the work I had done (to support the PAC study) and came up with the same figures for all the categories, which pleased me. However, for their sake, I am glad they also found an entire asset category that the internal auditor and I had overlooked. It was not large, but it was significant.

Costing the portfolio

With a reasonable handle on the physical state of assets, including quantity and quality, the next step was to calculate the replacement cost of the assets. Fortunately, the EWS had an estimations branch, whose job was to determine the approximate cost of any renewal or extension project the department was engaged in. This is where I realised the second of the two key advantages of being an economist. The first, as noted above, was that I naturally looked at the big picture and was happy to work with assumptions and approximations, whereas engineers are trained to pay attention to the details. The second was that not being an engineer, I was given leeway to ask idiotic questions, and I made full use of this.

My first idiotic question: 'How much does it cost to replace a kilometre of pipe?'

The patient response: 'What size pipe?'

'I don't know; what sizes do you have?'

He showed me a very long list of every size of pipe in the portfolio, along with the number of kilometres for each.

There were a handful of sizeable lengths and a much larger number with only a few kilometres each, so I said, 'Let me have the cost for each of these separately, and then you can give me an average for the rest.'

'OK. In the city or the country?'

'Does it make a difference?'

'Sure it does. In the city, we've got to work around lots of traffic, dig up and replace sealed roads, and work around an entire spaghetti of underground pipes and cables. The country is much easier, and we can often use the large earthmovers we can't use in the city.'

'I understand. So give me the costs separately for both city and country.'

'Will do. Now,' [with a wicked grin on his face] '... through rock or sand?'

If he hadn't grinned, I would have been stumped, since I didn't know how to tell which would apply. Instead, I said, 'Do you generally know before you get there?'

He admitted they generally didn't.

'So, what do you do?'

'We take an average.'

'Exactly! Then please take an average.'

We then dealt with sewers, pumps, dam renovations, and treatment stations.

Those guys were so patient with me, and I got excellent service from all the engineers that I dealt with. They were very bright, and I think they found dealing with an idiot like me a novelty. Dealing with a female was certainly a novelty. I was the only one in the entire department who was not a secretary, typist, or tea lady.

The final reckoning

At the beginning of this exercise in April 1984, most assumed that the value of our assets was around $800 million. No one knew, of course, because capital was not recorded, but this was the amount of debt the Treasury had 'allocated' to us and on which we paid interest. So, we reckoned that if we had $800 million of debt, we must have at least $800 million of assets. That is what most assumed if they thought about it at all — and generally, they didn't.

Not until we started looking into it. Then some thought it could be a bit higher and estimated $1 billion. Alan Herath, my boss, thought it could be as much as $3 billion; the others laughed at this, but he was the closest.

The final figure, the replaceable value of our assets, was $8 billion, ten times the figure that most had initially assumed! The written-down value was roughly two-thirds of this, but the replaceable value, of course, was what was relevant for asset management.

How could it be so much more than our allocated debt figure? There were a few reasons: one, the allocation was just that, an allocation — it bore no relevance to asset values; two, we had, from time to time, repaid some of the allocated debt whenever Treasury had requested it; three, it was a historical figure and did not represent current values.

These things, however, were dwarfed into insignificance by the amount of our asset stock that the Treasury or the department had not funded and thus incurred debt for. A very large part of our asset stock, including the 359-kilometre Morgan–Whyalla overland pipeline constructed during the war years, was funded by a Commonwealth grant. The 1960s saw the second of the large overland pipelines constructed. In addition, at this time, when new suburbs were being developed at a rapid rate, developers would construct the necessary roads, water and sewer networks and then pass them back to the government to be maintained in perpetuity. All of these 'gifted' assets were valued in our books at a nominal 'place-holding' of one dollar!

Once we had reasonable current replacement capital estimates, this was not the end. To answer our initial question, we still needed to calculate annual capital costs, which required determining the rate at which our assets were being consumed (either by wear and tear or obsolescence), and we needed to consider the opportunity cost of having so much money invested in these capital assets.

So that's what I did next, and that gave us the opportunity to move on to our second question.

We called our study The True Cost Study. This was not taken kindly by the CFO (Chief Financial Officer), who thought it reflected poorly on him. Such was not our intention; we simply needed a term to differentiate our figures from those in the financial records.

CHAPTER 2

CALCULATING THE COST AND TIMING OF INFRASTRUCTURE RENEWAL

As we gathered the information and understanding to answer question 1, we found that we could do more. We could go beyond measuring what it cost today, and look ahead to what it might cost to sustain our infrastructure and when, or to consider future renewal, asking:

Q 2: WHAT WILL IT COST TO REPLACE AGEING WATER ASSETS AND WHEN WILL THIS LIKELY OCCUR?

Life-cycle modelling

Now that we had a handle on our total asset portfolio, its size, age distribution, and estimated economic lives, the next step was to look to the future.

The engineering study commissioned by the department for its underground assets concluded that no major renewal would be needed for its underground assets for about fifteen years. The True Cost modelling confirmed this and extended it to the above-ground assets. But our modelling also enabled us to look beyond the fifteen-year mark to determine that around this time, or the year 2000, the amount of renewal falling due would begin to rise and, once begun, it would continue to rise.

At this stage, only the city's pipes and sewers had been replaced, and that was not because of age but because the city was increasing beyond the system's initial capacity. Just about all other assets were in their first 'asset life'. That meant that not only did we not know how long they would last but that, over time, a larger and larger proportion of the portfolio would become due for renewal.

The initial commissioned report that examined the department's underground assets had provided comfort by saying they were fit for the next fifteen years. Since this was a long time away, most extrapolated it to everything and for all time, certainly for their working lives. So, I took to illustrating our results dramatically by sweeping my hand across the table and declaring, 'There is no problem for the next fifteen years', then allowing my hand to drop precipitously off the edge!

Life-cycle modelling had long been a technique for comparing proposed investment projects with different cost and benefit timeframes. We would simply discount all the amounts back to the present and compare the net present values (NPV). It was a technique well-known to the department. So, to project likely renewal, I took the life-cycle framework, but instead of discounting back to the present to get a figure at one point in time, I focused on developing the most reliable distribution of future-component renewal costs. Since we were not funding the future, merely trying to establish what it would be, no discounting was needed or applied.

The importance of asset-age distributions

But of course, our assets were not new, so we could not assume, as we would if we were making an NPV comparison, that all were at the beginning of their cycles. We needed to allow for where each system and component was in its own life cycle. To do this, we sought to establish when each pipeline, sewer, or above-ground structure was established.

Fortunately, as we saw in Chapter 1, the engineers in charge had been with the department for many years and could make reasonable judgements on these start dates. They also knew when major changes affected asset-life profiles. For example, during the war years, most of the first-class materials and workers were taken up in the war effort, and the assets constructed during those years were already showing signs of earlier renewal requirements than the pre-war assets.

And again, later, when pipes and sewers for the new suburban developments began to be designed and constructed by developers, to be then handed back to the department for ongoing maintenance, it was discovered, not surprisingly, that these assets also had shorter timeframes. So, we segmented the asset distribution into pre-war, wartime, post-war, but before suburban development, and more recent years, and then constructed model variations for each.

We modelled in five-year segments. To pretend to be any more precise than this would have been ridiculous. Sometimes we could be quite accurate in pinpointing which five-year bracket applied; at other times, we knew only within ten or twenty years and needed to take an educated guess. The appropriate life-cycle model was then applied to each five-year age cohort within each asset class, allowing for model variants.

The complete model, with all data, assumptions and details, along with discussion and recommendations, can be found in the *PAC Report on Water Asset Renewal* (available on the Talking Infrastructure website at www.talkinginfrastructure.com/tams).

Modelling assumptions

Some assumptions had to be made to support the modelling, but we tried to make as few controversial judgements as possible. So, the first thing we did was to model everything in terms of current values. These we knew. Of course, prices would be expected to change over the course of the projection, but there was no way of knowing how. We certainly didn't want the logic of our model to be lost in a fruitless discussion of what future inflation was likely to be.

Next, we assumed that everything we had we would replace, and what's more, we would replace it like-for-like. Now, this is clearly not a good practice for actual renewal, but this default simplified the modelling — indeed, it made it possible.

We also assumed the same maintenance and renewal practices that we were currently using. Moreover, we would not assume that some miracle would occur with technology that would solve our future renewal problems or that prices would marvellously change in our favour. We kept those factors constant. In other words, we didn't want to assume away the future problems we were likely to face.

One other thing we did, which was exceedingly important, was that whenever there was any doubt about a future cost, we would take the lowest figure. This we stated upfront. We knew the projections would be scary enough, even when understated, and we didn't want the results to be dismissed as overstatements.

The 'abatement factor'

This is not to say that there was not considerable dispute along the way before we settled on these assumptions.

One of the arguments favoured by a section of the engineers was the 'abatement factor'. They argued, reasonably, that it was quite likely that over the next fifteen years and more, there would be technological improvements and price changes. Moreover, these could reduce the future price by as much as 20%, said some; others argued as much as 50%.

My response was, 'While we are guessing, what about 100%?'

That, however, was considered truly absurd.

The important point was that if we were to write down the size of our future renewal problem by assuming that lots of technological change applying to renewal would take place anyway, why would we bother to undertake the technical research to make it happen? Moreover, as we looked around at that stage, most technologies seemed to be applied to new assets rather than replacement assets.

Fortunately, the renewal problem was not written away on paper, and new and exciting techniques of renewal were developed as the extent of future demand became clearer.

The point of future renewal projections is not to be accurate predictors but to provide guidance so that decision-makers can take action to change the default future. If the renewal projections were to 'come true', they would have failed to do their job!

Asset consumption

The most difficult parts of the model to estimate were the rate of asset consumption and the opportunity cost. The reason these were difficult is that they ran afoul of current financial practices.

Infrastructure assets at that stage did not feature in the financial accounts and were not depreciated. Nevertheless, they still wore out or became obsolete, and we needed to account for this when we calculated what it cost to supply water and sewer services to South Australians. It was, of course, equally critical in determining future costs.

At the time, asset consumption was represented by a sinking fund. However, the sinking fund was calculated in historical cost terms, and when we looked at the amounts that were being set aside (generally as a gentlemen's agreement between the finance section of the EWS and the Treasury), the figure would only be appropriate if all our assets lasted more than 350 years! Our modelling figures were based on the engineers' expected life figures and replacement costs.

Opportunity costs

Opportunity costs were even more difficult, principally because, if you weren't an economist, you probably didn't know what they were. These are the costs that we were incurring for South Australia by investing in large-scale water infrastructure rather than investing in whatever the next best opportunity would have been.

Now, we didn't know this figure, but we did know that it wasn't zero. For the EWS, the figure that came closest to this (although not very close) was the interest amount that the Treasury charged on their allocation of debt to us. This was loosely informed by the interest rates that the Treasury was using in its cost–benefit analyses for new projects. This was also a matter of dispute between the engineers.

In my first few weeks with the department, I attended an Engineering Society meeting that was being addressed by a former economics lecturer of mine, who had subsequently become Minister for Education, and in whose electoral campaign I had participated. At this meeting, he argued that the discount factor (i.e., the interest rate that the Treasury was using) was too high and should be down around 2%. My engineering colleagues loved it and agreed.

At the time, I thought this was wrong and preferred the Treasury's higher figure, but now I am inclined to think he had right on his side. I am still not entirely convinced because, if this were the only, or key, deciding factor, the lower the interest rate, the more infrastructure projects are likely to be accepted, and investment could be overdone. Arguably, it should not be the only factor, but that is for a later volume in this series.

The size of the asset portfolio

As we calculated the size of the asset portfolio, the engineers got excited. A sort of shadow — unstated but well-known — competition was taking place, and I was always being bailed up as I waited for the lift or ate in the cafeteria to know what the 'latest figure' was. The CEO and Deputy CEO were not immune from the fun of seeing the figure rise. The higher it went, the happier they were because it reflected well on them, bolstering their importance to the organisation.

The same, however, was not true of accounting and finance. Their situation, of course, was entirely different. The larger the replacement value, the more difficult their future financial problems would be. It also became harder, even impossible, to reconcile our figures with those in the financial records.

Finance sought to defend what they had been doing rather than recognising that we now had a chance to fill in some of the gaps in our knowledge. Moreover, The True Cost Study made it clear that a lot of what we had been taking for granted as 'costs' were, in fact, merely a cosy and long-standing gentlemen's agreement between our finance people and those in the state Treasury, so it was to be expected that, in presenting the results of our work to the Executive Committee, we would get a lot of opposition from finance.

Presentation to the Executive Committee

When it eventually came time to present the new True Cost approach to the Executive Committee, I ran a rehearsal with my corporate planning colleagues. Every few minutes, they would stop me and say, 'But if you say that, then the CFO will …'. I realised that I could be walking into a minefield.

However, I took notice of everything they said and, on the day, anticipated the CFO's reaction by saying, whenever I came to one of the points that I had been warned about, 'Well of course, a possible reaction might be … but clearly this can be addressed by …'. Or 'Some might say … but we can readily recognise that this cannot be the case because ...'. Or something similar.

My colleagues had done a wonderful job in identifying all the CFO's objections, and he was getting more and more frustrated as I moved through the presentation until, at last, he couldn't take it anymore and burst out, 'But if we do what you suggest, we will become more efficient and have to sack people.' I meekly confessed that I had not foreseen this outcome! But by this time, there were grins all around the room, and I knew we had won.

(Incidentally, a few years later, the CFO made a presentation to the Engineering Society claiming that he had been responsible for the entire approach and was then rather sheepish when he realised that I was in the audience. But I didn't mind. If he could boast about it, he would take it on board.)

We are not alone

After the results of our modelling had been accepted by the executive, showing we had a period of grace of about fifteen years before our renewal requirements would start to rise, I suggested to the CFO that we could use that time to devise our renewal funding strategy.

He told me he had his own strategy: 'When we need extra funding, I simply ring the Treasury and say "Fred, we need another $50 million," and Fred says, "OK, you've got it."'

I was astonished and said that it was likely there would come a time when no matter how much the Treasury was onside, Fred would be financially unable to say, 'You've got it', but the CFO just shook his head at my woeful ignorance. This confirmed my understanding not only of the gentlemen's agreement but also how much it was leaving the department, and indeed the state, unprepared for change.

It led directly to my next question. We would not be the only department experiencing ageing infrastructure, so what demands, and when, would other departments be putting on Fred's largesse?

Question 3 thus became, 'What is the future cost and timing of all of the state's infrastructure?' with a natural follow-on as Question 4, 'What can be done to manage this cost?'

I had started to do a few back-of-the-envelope calculations based on conversations with engineers from other departments when, unexpectedly, an opportunity arose that I would have been mad not to take — although, at the time, I did my best to avoid it! But we will continue that story in Chapter 4. Let us look now at the reactions to The True Cost Study within the department and the water industry.

CHAPTER 3

REACTIONS

The right time and place

Had I tried to do this exercise anywhere else than with the EWS, I am now convinced it would not have seen the light of day. I would have been blocked by those who foresaw their current situation changing in ways they could not control.

Chief amongst these was finance, as was later to be confirmed by the reactions of the state Treasury. There really was nothing in this exercise for finance. They were comfortable with the way things were. They knew what they were doing and had 'the power of the purse'. What I was proposing was going to shake things up.

Finance has a short-term focus, mostly on the current budget year and next year's budget bid. Engineers are able to take a longer-term view, and fortunately, engineers were dominant in the EWS. They were excited to realise that their asset portfolio was so big and, thus, important! So, regardless of personalities, it was natural that I would get more support from engineering than from finance. But, of course, there was more involved. There always is.

Small things can have large consequences

I am English, and the English are particular about their tea. I did not care for the brew that was served from the large urns in the basement café, so although the CEO's secretary had declared that the tearoom on our executive floor was for the sole use of the CEO and his guests, early in my time with the EWS, I decided to disregard this and make myself a cup of tea with fresh hot water.

As I was doing so, the CEO himself arrived and so, caught, what could I do but smile brightly and say, 'Would you like a coffee?' I made him a coffee and was about to take my tea back to my room when he said, 'No, come and talk to me.' He was curious to know what economists did and what they could contribute to his department, and so, in those first few weeks, I often had morning tea with the CEO.

I guess these conversations might have given him the impression I knew something about politics, although I hardly did, for one morning, he interrupted one of our corporate planning meetings with 'Good morning, Penny and gentlemen, and it's you I want.' Naturally, my mind immediately leapt to what transgressions I might have committed. Fortunately, he just wanted help.

The irrigators had not taken kindly to the latest price rise, and they had come, en masse, with their equipment, blocking exits from Parliament House and demanding to speak with the minister, who wasn't at all keen to speak with them.

When the CEO told me what was up, I said, in exasperation, 'My goodness, water is really a small part of their budget when compared to electricity, and the electricity price goes up every year and much more than water, yet I don't see them complaining about that!'

'Is that true?'

'Yes, sure, look at this,' and I showed him the spreadsheet I was working on, which displayed the proportion of different expenses within a typical irrigator's budget. He was delighted, and promptly got through to the minister, who, now armed with a few facts, came out and addressed the motley assemblage.

Later the CEO made me his Executive Officer. Although I chafed at what I initially saw as a menial chore, the position not only allowed me to observe a master strategist up close but also enabled me to develop good relations with all the public service heads. This little thing turned out to be useful later when I needed to get them onside with the work I was to do with the parliament.

Take every opportunity you can — you never know when it will make a difference

A few weeks into my term with the EWS, my colleague, Rex, was meant to attend a meeting on the Water Resources floor but had an urgent job on — would I like to go instead? It was about measuring the level of salinity in the River Murray, of which I knew little, but I was happy to go.

When I got there, a consultant was reporting on his study of the costs of salinity along the Murray. The guy had measured salinity at its lowest and highest points and then had simply drawn a straight line between them, thus assuming that the costs of increasing salinity were linear.

Without thinking much about it, I asked him for the whiteboard marker. Surprised, he gave it to me, and I drew another line on the board, one that inclined very slowly at the beginning and then started to increase until it met the highest point. I pointed out that salinity costs do not rise immediately because the river can cope with a certain amount of salinity, so drawing the curve the way he had would overstate salinity costs all along the river and, importantly, it would also miss identifying the point at which costs started to rise rapidly, even exponentially.

The consultant was furious. And fair enough. It had not been my intention to upstage him, but I had just left the university where, for the past ten years, I had been running economics tutorials in small rooms with a whiteboard just like this, and habit took over.

I would have immediately apologised and explained, but he gave me no chance, rounding on me and demanding belligerently to know how long I had been in the EWS.

'Just a few weeks,' I answered.

'Then what do you know about water?'

I admitted, 'Not much, but this really isn't a water problem, is it? It is a logic problem.'

This sent him up the wall, and he started to berate me. Fortunately, a glance at my watch reminded me that the branch was going out to lunch with the CEO, so I stood up, smiled at everyone and said, 'I'm sorry to leave you, but I have a luncheon engagement with the Chief.' (I omitted to say that the whole branch was going.)

This exchange enchanted the engineers in the Water Resources Division! Being a friend of the CEO, the consultant had won many commissions and would lord it over the departmental engineers, who felt they had little option but to put up with it.

When the word got around, the engineers on the Water Resources floor quickly and warmly welcomed me. They would tell me the problems they were wrestling with, and we would try to find solutions. I enjoyed their issues more than those in corporate planning so would spend a lot of time on that floor, and irrigation and salinity issues became what I was known for.

One thing led to another — as it always does

About a month later, I was asked to contribute a chapter in a report seeking financial support from the Commonwealth Government for correcting river salinity along the River Murray. South Australia was at the tail end of the river, so was most affected.

The other chapters were to be written by engineers, and I didn't want a report so important to the state to look as if it were a patched-up job, which it would if I wrote using economic terminology. So to ensure that my language matched theirs, I talked to each of the intending authors, whom by now I knew, about what I wanted to say. I noted what terms they used in response and used those terms in my chapter. This gained me the reputation of being 'the only economist who can write so that engineers can understand'!

Australian states are quite competitive. Getting New South Wales, Victoria and South Australia to cooperate on the salinity issue required a carrot. This would be greater funding support from the Commonwealth.

If each of the states were to contribute one-eighth and the Commonwealth could be induced to pick up the remaining five-eighths, they were prepared to work together. But what would convince the Commonwealth to be so generous?

I argued that it had an 'historical moral responsibility' (a term I invented). The salinity problem arose because of irrigation along the river, and this had been the result of the Commonwealth establishing returned soldiers on the land. That was a worthy objective, but we argued that the Commonwealth had benefitted, and it was now time for them to pay the costs.

These were all small things, but they garnered me a lot of support from my engineering colleagues. This did not stop them from arguing with me or critically assessing what we were later to do, but they were generally onside, and their criticisms were constructive.

With their help and the Chief's support, I achieved a lot, particularly since it was not my aim to take the credit. I just wanted to see the job through to a successful conclusion. In fact, at one stage, I happily told my boss that I could get anybody to do anything — I just had to let them take the credit for it. Alan replied softly that that might be so, but why would anyone fund corporate planning if everything was seen to be achieved elsewhere? A good point! I realised that my task-oriented focus was not strictly strategic, and that was a valuable lesson, albeit one that I had to re-learn several times.

Things did not start well with the CFO — the water price

I received an early black mark from the CFO. On my third day in the department, the conversation turned to the water price, which was about to be announced. The CFO held that there would be no increase that year. My role at that stage was to observe, and things would have been fine if that was all I had done.

However, I thought this result unlikely and explained why: an election had recently been held, and the incoming administration had campaigned on a promise not to raise any new rates or charges. So, as governments always want more money, it stood to reason that if new rates were out, they would need to increase the rates they already had.

Moreover, since there had been no rise in the water rate in the lead-up to the election, I figured it would be raised that year. The CFO was rather miffed that a newcomer should challenge his opinion and demanded brusquely, 'OK, then what will it be?'

Put on the spot, I suggested 5%, and that is what it turned out to be. Pure chance, of course. But from that moment on, the CFO and I were on a collision course.

From bad to worse — the castor story

When, about a month or so later, a castor came off my office chair, I said, as I surveyed the damage, 'I had better get this to the repair shop to get it fixed.'

At this, the others yelled, 'No! Don't do that! It will be cheaper to get a new chair.'

I laughed. But they were deadly serious. More than that, they were right! The repair shop had adopted the fashionable new policy of 'charging out', meaning they were able to charge other branches for the in-house work they did. This might have worked fine had they had any competition, but they hadn't. They could charge anything they liked.

Moreover, they had simplified their accounting by allocating all their monthly costs (including all their idle time, which was increasing by the month) over any jobs they had on hand. As their charges rose, jobs stopped coming in, causing the next round of price rises.

This had now reached the stage where having a castor re-attached would genuinely cost more than the chair itself. Yet no one had done anything about it!

Even worse, the chief accountant was so proud of his financial policy that he and the CFO were planning to run an international conference to show it off to the national and international water authorities. I explained what was wrong with this approach to my branch head and wrote two papers, one in the vernacular so that everyone could see how damaging it was, and the other in more measured academic terms. The conference was cancelled, so at least we did not look like an international laughingstock, but it did not win me any favours with the chief accountant or the CFO.

Changing the policy, however, was more difficult as accounting stuck its heels in and had the minister sign an instruction demanding that all jobs be sent to the repair shop. With the growing dominance of the 'free market competition' model across the country, this could be considered the public sector dipping its toe in the water, trying to become 'more efficient, more competitive, more market oriented', yet still wanting, and indeed having, to operate within a public sector framework.

There is no doubt I could have been more diplomatic, but I doubt the results would have been any different, for 'charging out' was to become the flavour of the month for many other departments. I spent many years when I became an infrastructure advisor either correcting the damage done or warning policymakers off.

The value of opposition

With hindsight, the CFO's opposition was extremely valuable. It stopped me from getting sloppy. I had to be forever on my toes, anticipating him wherever I could and dealing with him when I couldn't.

He had a clever way of blocking me without seeming to be in opposition. He would challenge me on every point I made, but if I was able to overcome that, he would proclaim that what I was doing was very important and that I should extend my inquiries to cover a wider field. By increasing the scope, he intended to slow me down. It was very effective.

He always sat opposite me at the meeting table, but one day I deliberately chose to walk around the table and sit next to him. He looked startled and, curiously, for that entire meeting he did not challenge a word I said. My reading on handling difficult people had suggested that this would be the case, but I didn't believe it until I tried it out for myself.

This was, of course, not the solution to all problems, but learning to deal with negative reactions was to prove very useful wherever I went.

The reaction of other water authorities

After I presented The True Cost Study to the executive committee, the CEO said, with a happy smile on his face, 'That was great. Now I want you to find out what everyone else is doing!'

Still flying from a successful presentation, I cheekily replied, 'Do you mean, get on the phone and find out or get on a plane and find out?' He then said what he was to repeat many times while I was in the department: 'Penny, you must do what you think fit.' So, I got on a plane.

I visited every mainland water authority except Darwin, and everywhere the story was the same: 'When do you say major renewal will start to ramp up? No problems! I will be retired by then!' For managers of very long-living assets, they took a very short-run view, mainly concerned with maintaining and renewing what they already knew to be substandard.

No one was looking out beyond five years and trying to anticipate where problems might arise. They did not have estimates of economic life, and the standard method for determining the time to intervene was the 'bathtub curve' familiar to all engineers and still practised in many places today. Namely, after a pre-determined number of breaks, the pipe or sewer would be replaced. There was no cost analysis. Because of this, all water authorities kept statistics on the number of breaks per kilometre.

In Sydney, I was given a polite hearing. They were tolerant rather than genuinely interested — until I told them our current break rate. It was the same as theirs, to the decimal point! Now this was pure coincidence, and nothing on which to base a decision, for the geography was entirely different.

Sydney has a hilly terrain to traverse; the land is flat in Adelaide. The current average number of breaks should have been irrelevant. Nevertheless, the fact that our break rate was identical to Sydney's changed the entire conversation. The same CEO who had previously declared that he would be retired before problems arose was now intensely interested. Sydney Water then became quite proactive.

In fact, as word of what we were doing spread in the water industry, there was a great deal of interest by all water authorities across the country, and water became the first industry to develop asset management (AM) skills. This then spread to contacts in water authorities overseas.

CHAPTER 4

MOVING ON — MY STORY

Public service advice

When I started in the public service, I was given a piece of advice that I thought, and still think, was sound. I was advised to spend about two to two-and-a-half years in three different agencies and then decide whether I wanted to remain in the public service or move on. This period was considered the optimal time for me to give what I could give and to learn what I needed to learn.

But good advice or not, I was enjoying my work with the EWS and did not want to leave. So, when the two-year mark arrived, I compromised and applied for a one-year secondment to the Public Accounts Committee. When the interview was due, however, and after I had deferred it for as long as possible, I wanted to change my mind.

Now, this may sound sexist, and it is, but at that time, and maybe still today, a male could say he'd changed his mind, and it would be accepted, but if you were female, the more likely response would be, 'She simply doesn't know her own mind', and it would have been a mark against her. Still, I reasoned, how hard can it be to fail an interview? And that's what I decided to do. On the day of the interview, I dressed down. Flat shoes. No makeup.

How not to fail an interview

That interview would have to be the weirdest I have ever taken. The interview panel comprised the Chairman of the Public Accounts Committee and one of his committee members, the Committee Secretary, the Speaker of the House, and his clerk. The Speaker introduced everyone to me and then picked up a newspaper and disappeared behind it for the rest of the hour, to be seen and heard no more.

I was polite and answered the questions as intelligently as I could. Then the committee member asked me how much work I did on programmed performance budgeting (PPB). Quite frankly, I did nothing and said so. The fellow coloured up immediately, and it was clear that he'd had a hand in getting the program adopted. 'Do you mean to say that the EWS is not taking PPB seriously?' he demanded.

I told him that there were two answers to his question. I then spoke of the assiduous work carried out by my colleagues in this area (which was a bit of an exaggeration) and, when he was breathing normally again, I reminded him that I had said there were two answers.

By this time, he was interested to know what the second answer was, so I told him. 'You realise, I suppose, that PPB cannot do what it is claimed it can do?' And he was off again! It was mean of me, but I told him of the problems that had been experienced interstate wherever it had been applied, and why we lacked both the data and the motivations for it to work.

That rather set the tone for the rest of the interview. Now, instead of polite questions, I was being challenged. Good. Things were going as intended.

The chairman asked me the difference between efficiency and effectiveness and whether the PAC was effective. I said, with a smile, that if he would tell me what his criteria for effectiveness were, I would be able to answer his question. I had taken a punt that he wouldn't have any criteria, and he didn't.

By this time, he knew I was playing with him, and I thought that should have been sufficient to scratch my name off the list. But my answer seemed to pique his interest. 'Tell me,' he said, 'what do you think we should be doing?'

And that was when the wheels came off my plan

I told him that there were two important problems that some parliamentary body should be looking at, and if it was not them, I didn't know who it could be. Now they were all interested.

I told him that through our Treasury, the South Australian Government Financing Authority had been very successful at acquiring funds (at a time of restriction through the Commonwealth Government's Global Loan Limits) because they were offering attractively high rates. However, this put the onus on them to find borrowers who would pay them even higher rates, and that had put us into a high-risk zone.

The other issue related to our ageing infrastructure and our unpreparedness for future renewal. I told them that, as the Public Accounts Committee, it was their responsibility to be aware of these consequences of government spending, but they had absolutely no idea of how much they would be up for, nor when such infrastructure renewal spending would fall due; no one did.

The committee chose to explore the debt issue for the remainder of the session, and we didn't come back to the renewal issue again. Even so, I had the distinct impression that I had failed at the simple act of failing an interview, and this was confirmed the following morning when my boss was informed that I had been chosen. There was just one last opportunity to get myself out from under as they wanted to have a longer conversation with me that morning in the House.

At this meeting, I told them I knew nothing about politics and would not even recognise the eminent members I passed in the House. Talk about digging a deeper hole! Too late, I realised that ignorance is a good substitute for impartiality in a bipartisan committee researcher.

My research had shown me that the PAC's practice up to now was to do small investigations, which I referred to as 'pinging' exercises, such as identifying and penalising low-level officers for the misuse of government cars. This was of no interest to me.

I told them that I would not investigate my department, the EWS. Fair enough, they said. Moreover, I would not investigate the agriculture department. This puzzled them. Why not? I explained that I had, over the past eighteen months, built a good rapport within this department, a rapport that was very useful for the government work that I was doing in irrigation pricing and water transfers and that I did not want to ruin it for the sake of a one-year secondment. OK, they said.

Damn! What could I do now?

An opportunity too good to refuse

Then a very interesting change took place. I realised that they did not have any of the traditional pinging exercises in mind for me, but that I was, in fact, being offered a chance to take the infrastructure renewal work that I had done for the EWS and expand it to cover all the major infrastructure holdings in the state.

'Can you do this in one year?' they asked.

I thought this highly unlikely, but what I said was, 'I will give it a go.' It ended up taking just over two and a quarter years.

Any academic researcher will appreciate the enormous opportunity this presented. I would do a research project of my own choosing, be paid very well for doing it, and be supported by the committee's Royal Commission powers, which would ensure I got all the information I wanted. I stopped trying to get myself out from under and said yes!

There was an additional benefit that I did not recognise at the time. That was the opportunity to get the results of the work out into the wider world owing to the credibility that comes from parliamentary reports.

Why had the committee decided to depart from tradition and do a research project? Well, of course, it was intrigued by the idea of doing something more significant than its usual exercises.

It also happened that the PAC was headed up not only by a very intelligent chairman but also an extremely capable secretary, and I suspect that the secretary, with whom I had spoken before applying for the position, had had a word with the committee members to get them onside with the idea of doing a research project.

Then there was the timing. A new election was due within about six months, and the government members (who were the majority on the committee) did not want any government failings to be brought up in the media in the lead-up to the election. The fact that I would be unable to produce anything before the election was thus in my favour.

Had I been more successful at failing interviews, I would have missed the opportunity to take the back-of-the-envelope calculations I had been working on and develop the information base needed if the parliament and government were to take future renewal seriously.

End Note

As a side issue, I later learnt that, after the interview, the Speaker of the House came out from behind his newspaper and said, 'We'll have her! If she is asked to stick the knife in, she will only ask "how far?"' I think he was referring to my exchange with the committee member over PPB. I like to think that the chairman had a different reason for choosing me; he liked to provoke me into argument, which we both enjoyed, and later he offered me the position of his chief of staff when he was made Minister for Energy, so perhaps he had.

PART TWO: EXPLORATION

FEBRUARY 1985– APRIL 1987

THE PUBLIC ACCOUNTS COMMITTEE

In the second part of this volume, I look at the questions that occupied me when I worked with the Public Accounts Committee of the South Australian Parliament and was tasked with taking the work that I had done with the Engineering and Water Supply Department of South Australia and extending it to all major infrastructure agencies in the state.

CHAPTER 5

PROJECTING RENEWAL FOR OTHER INFRASTRUCTURE AGENCIES

On observing, in Chapter 2, that the Chief Financial Officer in the EWS believed that renewal money would simply appear whenever he needed it, it seemed likely that other agencies might also think that way. So, with all agencies experiencing infrastructure ageing and with the invaluable support of the parliamentary PAC and its Royal Commission-style information-gathering powers, it was time to ask:

Q 3: WHAT IS THE FUTURE COST TO THE STATE OF ALL MAJOR INFRASTRUCTURE RENEWAL?

Framing the question

Developing and arguing the concepts of The True Cost Study and applying them to the water authority to create, in effect, an asset management 'proof of concept' had been great fun. Engineers and economists tend to think alike, as a leading New Zealand accountant once explained to me apropos my frustration with accountants: 'If you have a problem, you go back to first principles, don't you?'

'Of course!'

'Yes, and so do engineers, but accountants ask, "What's the rule?"'

I laughed when I first heard this, but recognised the truth of it and the necessity for it. Now, at the PAC, the question was: how do politicians think?

The answer is that they are more sensitive to public reactions. In fact, more sensitive overall. When I said, during one board meeting, that I was not a member of the public service union, they all turned on me, and Heini Becker, a right-wing politician, said, 'I'm not one of them, but even I am a member of my union!' That was an awkward moment, and I claimed — and they were prepared to accept for the sake of saving face — that my membership of the Economics Society was equivalent.

Economists also tend to deal with problems more neutrally and objectively than politicians. Indeed, emotional or 'coloured' language in economic argument is frowned on. To an economist, if there are two prices, you can refer to the lower as a 'discount' relative to the higher or the higher as a 'premium' relative to the lower, and the analysis is the same — just two different but related prices and either can express the relationship between them. Not to a politician, as I discovered when talking about electricity prices. A recent rise in the price had created much public dissension. So, it was fine to talk about discounts but definitely not safe to talk about premiums.

Overall, it was now necessary to present arguments, not for efficiency and effectiveness, as I had done in the water authority, but rather for parliamentary accountability and avoidance of waste. As we were a bipartisan committee, it was also necessary to avoid casting blame on any particular administration. This was easy, as the problem we were facing had been developed over at least the last forty years and many administrations. Instead, I aimed to create a sense of responsibility for correcting this long-standing problem, and the fact that the PAC was leading in a new and innovative field didn't hurt!

The Public Accounts Committee Inquiry

Over 1986 and 1987, we produced seven individual agency studies and a final summary report showing the impact on the whole state. The agencies we worked with were initially rather offended at our approach of treating them all on a common basis, for this challenged their deeply ingrained belief that each was 'different' and 'unique'.

However, it turned out to be a strength of the study. Not only did it enable aggregation, but results couldn't be disregarded as 'exceptions' relating to only one agency. It also led to the development of the general principles that were to become the basis of asset management, and agencies were later able to reassure themselves that they were not the only ones facing asset management challenges.

Our first agency study was public housing. This revealed that the Housing Trust was seriously unsustainable in the long term and, despite protests, even over the next ten years. As neither the South Australian State Government nor the Commonwealth was prepared to increase financial support, the Housing Trust found itself needing to downsize significantly. The issues, problems, and attitudes we discovered in this first study were to show up in all subsequent studies: for electricity, water, highways, hospitals, public transport, and education. Together, these agencies accounted for over 80% of all state infrastructure.

Our objective was to be able to forecast the extent of infrastructure renewal that would fall due in future years if we made no changes to our practices. A simple enough question, but we found that asset management extended far beyond the consideration of asset maintenance and renewal. As the following case study of public housing shows, we needed to consider not only portfolio sustainability but also financial management, demand management, market analysis, agency culture, and more.

A case study — public housing

The Housing Trust could not understand why we were looking at their long-term renewal.

'We have already carried out a complete audit of our housing portfolio. We know what the problems are, and we have a plan to address them over the next twenty years.'

My follow-up question, 'What of the problems that will only become evident over those next twenty years?', was met with genuine puzzlement.

But while the staff were merely puzzled, the CEO was quite antagonistic.

The committee had arranged for me to brief each agency CEO to explain that this was not a typical bad-practice investigation but rather a research activity to provide planning information for the South Australian Parliament. For most, the briefing went smoothly, but not so with the Housing CEO. He hardly let me get a word out before telling me, in a tone of considerable annoyance and stress, 'I don't have time to talk to you! I have a much more pressing problem. I need to convince the federal government it is on the wrong track in requiring current-value depreciation.'

As a statutory authority, the Housing Trust maintained accrual accounts, and its assets were recorded on its balance sheet. But they were in historical cost terms, which, after many years of high inflation, greatly understated current value. The federal government now wanted depreciation recorded on a current-value basis, which meant that these cost figures would be greatly increased.

The CEO was a worried man. In common with other agencies, he tended to act as if costs that were not recorded were not, in fact, incurred. Also, if depreciation costs were increased, he would need to increase rents unless the government provided greater support. He resisted.

As the federal government co-funded the Trust, it was entitled to ask for this information, but it had never done so before — so why now?

The answer lay in the economic reform mentioned in Chapter 1.

Economic reform

When the Australian Labor Party formed government in 1983, it had already learnt a major lesson from Gough Whitlam's shortened term in office a few years earlier, when, despite major social and environmental advances, Labor and the Left had lost their majority because of economic blunders. Labor leader Bill Hayden had warned that they needed to develop better economic management skills if they wanted to regain power — that is, skills superior to those of their opposition. So, economics took centre stage and, by 1985, two years into the administration, the scene was set for change.

And change we got. In abundance! For the past eighty years, the traditional Labor belief had been that the marketplace should be constrained by public controls on capital and interest rates and that there should be strong trade unions with a welfare system that ensured decent wages and support for the disadvantaged. In the next decade, everything changed. Markets were opened to the world, tariffs were abandoned, and the dollar was floated. Australia decided it was strong enough to trade freely in the global economy.

Thus, asset management developed at a time when the federal government was prepared for Australia to be an engaged member of the international economy. It was prepared to face the truth.

This environment was particularly hard on the Housing Trust, for while it had a business framework, it did not see itself as a business. It saw itself as a social institution caring for the homeless and disadvantaged. It focused on service and paid less attention to costs, having the view that what it did was so important that the funding, whatever it was, just needed to be provided.

It was very noticeable in the Trust, but this attitude of 'importance' justifying costs was common to all agencies at this time. The economic reforms led to pressure to identify costs, manage resource use, and plan for future sources of revenue.

Using or managing assets?

The Housing Trust didn't manage 'assets'; it managed the 'allocation of accommodation'. For this, it only needed to know where the house or unit was, how many bedrooms it had, and how easy it was to access. It did not record age, economic life, or replacement value, and it didn't know why these were of interest to us.

This was, in fact, true of all seven agencies. They acquired assets, operated and maintained them — that is, they used them — but they didn't 'manage' them. They kept only the information needed to provide current services, just as the Housing Trust did. They did not seek information to provide for future requirements or to ensure that assets were provided efficiently and effectively.

Until now, demand had been automatically met by increased supply. Alternatives had not been sought. Looking back, we might see it as a failure of stewardship and foresight, but it is important to remember that the asset management tools we have today did not exist then.

Our asset-management-related questions seemed not only strange but impossible to answer: How could anyone assign an age to a house with sixty-year-old foundations and a ten-year-old roof, that was rewired fifteen years ago and had just had its wet areas replaced and enhanced? How could anyone determine its current replacement value or its rate of asset consumption? But that is what we needed to do.

When the housing report was published showing that the Trust was unable to sustain its portfolio, the corporate planning staff were shocked. Naturally, for the results were indeed both serious and shocking. But they were also mystified. They didn't know how it could have happened and even doubted it had happened. In any case, how did we know? I pointed out that the asset values, rates of consumption, and likely future renewal, which were the basis of our conclusions, were all derived from their own Trust data.

'All the data came from you!' I told them. They agreed. 'Yes, but we didn't know you were going to do that with it!'

Modelling housing renewal

So, what was it that we did? We looked at their assets as 'assets' and built a model that could forecast the default future of housing renewal. Firstly, we calculated a unit cost replacement value for a typical Housing Trust house. Then we identified the key renewable components, their cost, their life, and their proportion of the total value.

This was a time-consuming process with much number crunching, necessitating many weeks on my hands and knees hovering over multiple years of the Trust's budget papers, contract payment documents, and other official papers spread all over the conference room floor. This was supplemented with quantity surveyors' estimates and the research findings of the Commonwealth Scientific and Industrial Research Organisation's (CSIRO) Division of Housing and Building Construction, plus many hours of conversation with the maintenance personnel.

The upshot was that we were able to identify 23 components and sub-components in the basic model. Lastly, we calculated the age distribution of the portfolio. The *PAC's 44th Report on Housing Asset Replacement* (available on the Talking Infrastructure website at www.talkinginfrastructure.com/tams) provides all the data we used, the basic model, its model variations, the assumptions we made and why we made them, along with the references we used to support them. We took the same approach for each agency.

Creating our own definitions

As our work was new, we were not surprised to find a lack of definitions, not only for asset management but for the infrastructure assets themselves. We needed to create our own. The committee took the view that a good definition gets the job done — or that 'purpose determines definition'.

Given our objective, we defined an infrastructure asset in terms of the treatment needed to provide services over the long term. Infrastructure was thus defined for our purposes as 'an asset with an undefined life kept operational as long as required by the piecemeal renewal of components'.

This enabled us to omit such short-lived assets as motor vehicles (typically renewed every two years according to federal tax remits) or computers, and to deal only with complex, multi-component, long-lived assets.

We also re-defined 'economic life' to suit such multi-component assets, and this became 'the time it takes for the cost of component renewal to equal the initial asset cost'. (This was defined, for consistency with our analysis, in real or current value, terms.)

These definitions remained in common use around the world for almost twenty years and are still more practical than some more modern 'general purpose' definitions intended to serve multiple uses.

When we deliberately choose definitions according to a specific purpose, it becomes clear that when we change our purpose, we need to reconsider and change our definitions as well. We may now wish to do this as we seek to drive infrastructure decisions that are 'fit for the future' and take environmental considerations into account.

The sustainable size of an asset portfolio

We used an estimate of one hundred years for those elements of a house likely not to be renewed until such time as the entire house is sold and replaced, such as foundations, walls and the roofing structure. Together with the individual component lives that we had calculated for the shorter living components, such as floor coverings, electrical appliances and the electric/gas service, we could determine the annual rate of asset consumption for public housing at 1.87%. In other words, roughly every 53.5 years, component renewal would amount to the total initial cost of the house (in current value terms). The 'annual rate of asset consumption' was a new concept for housing. It was not depreciation, which is a financial cost allocation, but rather an estimate of physical degradation and obsolescence.

Asset managers are now very familiar with these concepts and what they enable us to do — namely, to determine the sustainable level of an asset portfolio given the amount allocated for renewal. But this was the first time that information had been used in this way, hence the reaction of the Corporate Planning Branch: 'We didn't know you were going to do that with it!'

Knowing that it cost 1.87% of the value of the housing stock each year just to sustain it enabled us to establish the maximum portfolio that could be maintained with the renewal funds available, and the Trust's housing stock already greatly exceeded this level. This meant that unless the state or the Commonwealth (or both) was prepared to provide more — and neither was — the implication for the Trust was that it would need to reduce its portfolio. This was hard for the Trust to hear, for they already felt that they did not have enough housing and were planning large increases.

Making our challenges visible

Before our modelling, this situation had been invisible to the Trust. The level of maintenance and component replacement is generally low in the early years of a portfolio. For housing, it starts to become significant when houses reach around thirty to forty years of age.

In 1985, only a small proportion of the housing stock was in this high renewal-cost age bracket. But a major cohort, representing the Trust's post-war expansion, was about to move into this bracket within the next five to ten years. It was the ability of our modelling to project these future requirements that was to be so important for all agencies. And so scary!

These projections arose from taking a longer-term view and had very serious consequences. It was important to take all possible steps to confirm and communicate the accuracy of the modelling. Fortunately, the Trust itself helped make this possible.

It had been the practice of the Trust (and indeed most agencies) to include much component replacement, even upgrading to present standards, in the category 'maintenance expenditure' with insufficient detail to separate renewal from general, or routine, maintenance. However, by 1984–85, rapidly increasing levels of maintenance requests (the leading edge of future replacement increases) had led to quite detailed maintenance budgeting being prepared and, when examined, this enabled a replacement estimate to be determined for that financial year of $14.7 million, which was reassuringly close to the $14.6 million that the model projected for that period.

'Unfair and immoral'

The PAC had reserved its interpretations for its final report, wanting first to see the big picture, and so had not referred to the future sustainability problems in the housing report, including just the facts. Nevertheless, the significance of these facts was not lost on the head of the Trust. I was accused of artificially setting the life of a house far too short.

'Why, in England, there are thatched-roof cottages that are still fit after 350 years!' he declared, as if this somehow clinched his argument.

My mind immediately flashed to the exorbitant re-thatching costs those heritage properties required, not to mention that some modern humans would have to stoop to enter, a condition I could not imagine Housing Trust clients willingly accepting. I did not say this. Instead, I suggested that he ask his regional managers what lives they would expect. We then took an average, and their component life figures were within a few months of mine every time. I was not surprised, for I had developed my estimates in consultation with them in the first place.

This still did not satisfy the head of the Trust. In his eyes, it was both 'unfair and immoral' to cost asset consumption (or depreciation, as he called it) on houses that were being provided for the underprivileged. 'After all, rich private owners don't have to pay depreciation!' he said, which of course is true — instead, they directly fund the wear and tear on their properties represented by such depreciation.

Affordable housing

What made it especially difficult for the Trust was that the government continually spoke of public housing as 'affordable housing', meaning affordable for those on a low income. However, without the government subsidising the cost, it simply wasn't. The head knew this. He knew the Trust's houses were not built to a different, more 'affordable' design. Indeed, they sought to make them indistinguishable from other dwellings. Council regulations worked to the same end. So the only way he could lower the rates to make them more 'affordable' — in the absence of publicly admitting to a subsidy, which was considered not politically acceptable — was the deliberate understatement of the real costs.

I could appreciate the anguish of the Trust head, even while he ranted at me. Our projections made it clear that not only would the Trust be financially unable to increase its stock, but it wouldn't even be able to maintain the portfolio it already had. The Trust head argued this completely ignored the community's need for housing. He pointed to his rising waiting lists to show that housing needs were not diminishing but, in fact, expanding.

Winning the lottery

While government investment in public housing was necessary if the needs of those on lower incomes were to be met, did the rising waiting lists really measure need? By June 1985, the Trust held a full 10% of the state's entire housing stock and over one-third of its rental market. As these figures greatly exceeded those of other states, one might expect the South Australian waiting lists to be far lower. But they weren't. Quite the reverse. The SA waiting lists were not only high but, despite large annual acquisitions by the Trust, still rising.

In his write-up, after we published the housing report, Des Colquhoun, a columnist for *The Advertiser*, Adelaide's morning newspaper, recalled that in the 1950s — when housing generally was in short supply, and the state was unable to cope with the influx of returned soldiers, immigrants and refugees — being granted a Housing Trust house was like 'winning the lottery'! What he didn't realise, and neither did the Trust, was that it still was!

Conscious of the acres of bleak housing estates in the northern region that had been built in a great hurry during the 1950s (many using green timbers and inferior ceiling insulation because the state was running out of materials), the Trust was keen to do better. It wanted social housing to be indistinguishable from privately owned dwellings nearby. Socially, this was no doubt a good idea. But the consequence for the waiting list was that now 'winning' the prize was not only more likely, given the high rate of expansion of the stock, but with the low rental price yet reasonably high quality of public housing, the prize itself was so much more attractive and worth waiting for, with the result that more people applied, and the waiting lists exploded.

A few years later, I was travelling in Queensland with an officer from the Queensland housing authority who proudly told me that the new minister had been increasing the housing budget after many years of neglect. 'And are your waiting lists now rising?' I asked him. Astonished, he said, 'Why yes, how did you know?'

Understanding the market

At this stage in our research, we were becoming keenly aware that asset management involved far more than timely and appropriate maintenance and renewal. And it was not only the impact of external factors on housing, but housing's own impact on the market that was relevant.

To reduce its waiting lists, the Trust decided to increase its annual acquisitions from 2,000 to 6,000 units. Unfortunately, housing construction was already at full stretch, and all builders were gainfully employed, so for the Trust to add to its stock, it had to entice builders away from other jobs. This resulted in rising prices and longer completion times — for the Trust and everyone else.

The Trust complained bitterly about this but did not see itself as the cause. It used its large demand to insist on the lowest prices, so producing for the Trust was always less profitable than for the general market. With general demand high, the Trust could only attract builders away from the general market by raising the prices it was prepared to offer. It was thus triggering the effect it complained about.

I tried to explain this to the PAC chairman when we met for our normal briefing before the weekly committee meeting. He was not interested: new housing was funded by the Commonwealth. 'That's Commonwealth money. Forget it!' he said dismissively. And I snapped, 'Commonwealth, be damned, that's our tax money, and they are wasting it!'

Hardly the way to talk to your boss. On this occasion, he had been delayed by a succession of meetings, and it was 8 pm before we met. We were both tired and hungry, and our tempers were short, which I like to think was the reason for his unusually brusque response and my rudeness.

Funding future renewal

However, after we had both calmed down, we sat down and talked about it and then about the related general problem of tied grants — that is, the money granted to the states but tied to decisions made by the Commonwealth Government. The Commonwealth, which had the major taxing powers, wished only to fund additional assets, not renewal. We could see that this would greatly hamper our ability to cope as our assets aged.

Christopher Jay, a senior reporter for the *Australian Financial Review*, had made a presentation to the PAC Biennial Conference the previous year, showing that the proportion of grant money from the Commonwealth was increasingly in the form of these tied grants, thus favouring the Commonwealth's own new projects. In the last few years, he had shown there had been a 9% switch in funding from untied to tied grants. This was reducing the funding available for renewal and worsening the problem by increasing new additions.

At the committee meeting the following day, the chairman laid out the case against the Housing Trust's purchasing actions with great clarity. Later, when it was time to write the final report, he wrote the section on untying state grants to enable the flexibility to manage renewal.

Incidentally, federal funding of new assets, with renewal being the responsibility of state or local governments, is a problem still affecting Australia and many other countries.

Coming to grips with the new costing models

It was not only the Housing Trust that had difficulty with the notion of full costs. Most agencies, and their customers, believed that depreciation should not be charged to current users since it was providing for future assets and future services. There were a couple of misperceptions in that argument. Firstly depreciation, or asset consumption, simply records a cost without providing a fund for anything. Secondly, where agencies do choose to include these costs in their charges, it is a charge for the use that current consumers are making of the asset, even if that use does not have to be made good till later.

Examples from the other agencies

When the water authority included the cost of asset consumption (the using up of assets) in the service charge for the mains and sewers the developers had passed over to them for management, homeowners who had recently bought their houses protested that they had already paid for the mains and sewers in their house price, and this was now requiring them to pay twice. It became known as the 'double dipping' argument, which lasted for years. Homeowners didn't see that it was like buying a car and then paying a regular charge to have it continuously serviced. Full-cost pricing is still not well understood.

While only the Housing Trust was in a dire situation with long-term sustainability, all agencies found they needed to adjust once their full costs were known. The Highways Department saw the future funding it would need if it continued to replace lesser-used country roads on the same timescale as more trafficked city roads, as had been their practice, and quickly set about reconsidering the need.

In the past, the rate of technological development had meant it was always preferable for the Electricity Trust to move to the latest-generation technology. Larger generators were much cheaper to operate. This situation was now changing. The rate of improvement in technology was slowing down, cost savings were diminishing, and the risks of having so much capacity tied up in one generator were greatly increasing. This meant that renewal, not previously a consideration, now became a viable option.

The State Transport Authority had assumed that the economic life of a bus was 12 years but, pressed by the committee to carry out proper analysis, it found the life to be 16 years. This meant that by replacing at 12 years, it had been wasting a good quarter of its expensive bus assets, which were all imported. This was happening at a time when the terms of trade were turning against us, increasing state costs. Moreover, to avoid keeping buses beyond their supposed 12-year economic life, the authority had deliberately reduced its ability to repair and extend the life of older buses by reducing the size and capability of their workshops. This resulted in buses waiting longer for maintenance and with more time out of commission. The neglect of a simple AM exercise, such as determining the appropriate economic life, thus created numerous costly problems.

The Health Commission realised that, rather than just replacing like with like, the greatly changed demand for its maternity hospital services, for example, enabled renewal with smaller, more efficient units. It also saved on insurance when it started to think in terms of component renewal rather than in terms of whole hospitals.

What we learnt

Asset management meant extending the range of considerations for each asset decision. It was no longer a case of simply matching supply to expected demand. Everybody learnt something valuable. And so did we.

We realised that all agencies shared a common mindset. They all acted as if costs that weren't recorded weren't incurred. This was pre-commercialisation and a forerunner of the adjustment problems to be experienced a few years later.

Now it was time to take everything we had learned and express it in a way that all agencies and governments could understand and learn from. That was the task of the final, or summary, report, the 53rd PAC report.

CHAPTER 6

MANAGING STATEWIDE INFRASTRUCTURE RENEWAL

The 53rd PAC Report provided the summary and did what the individual reports could not do — it looked at the aggregate renewal impact and compared the changing needs of different agencies over time. The high-cost renewal periods for different agencies (and for elements within agencies) would change over time so that the common maintenance budgeting approach of 'whatever you had last year, plus or minus a bit' wouldn't work. The pie charts in the summary PAC report made this abundantly clear. Attention needed to be paid to prioritisation according to need and to answer the more general question:

Q 4: HOW CAN WE CONTAIN THESE RENEWAL COSTS?

The purpose of projections

We had learnt a great deal in our examination of the seven agencies, but it quickly became evident that the real measure of success would be our ability to communicate and convince others to act.

'Do you swear by the accuracy of these figures?'

I was being grilled by consultants who had been called in by the Housing Trust, still resisting the changes it would need to make.

I laughed. 'Who will swear to the future? What I can say is that they are the best that can be done with present information. Moreover, even if the renewal figures are out by as much as 20% or even 30% — and I am quite confident that they are not — it would still make no difference to the actions the Trust now needs to take.'

The purpose of the projections for all agencies was to enable them to realise and make needed strategic-level changes. Fortunately, the Trust's consultants were astute enough to realise this and brave enough to convince their client of the new directions needed. The fact that all agencies needed to make changes actually helped each of them step forward and start to do what was needed.

Peaks and troughs

When we started, it had been an open question whether the renewal peaks of some agencies would nicely dovetail with the troughs of others and so enable increased requirements to be evenly distributed over time. This was the hopeful case. It was not to be. Peaks piled up on peaks. Default projections showed a pattern of renewals falling due that had already started to rise and would continue — rising to multiples of current levels before falling back a little but, overall, remaining many times higher than current levels.

This estimate was conservative and represented the lower bound of future renewal requirements. It only projected renewal of those assets held in

1985, did not include assets that agencies had continued to add, and only included the seven agencies the committee had examined. One notable omission was all the government office buildings that were not in our seven agencies.

What was true for public housing — that it now had young asset portfolios with low maintenance and renewal requirements compared with what would be needed later — was true for all infrastructure. A major post-war infrastructure expansion between the 1950s and the early 1970s had led to rapid population growth. Not only were new suburbs continually spreading, but the capacity of existing towns and suburbs was being exceeded. The city and older suburban water services required radical renewal and new technology, such as copper wiring replacing older electricity distribution wires, was impacting renewal.

Between growth and technology change, most infrastructure portfolios in 1985 were still young. Almost all organisations projected future renewal needs by extrapolating from current maintenance and renewal requirements, leading to serious underestimation.

Agencies that were beginning to experience the leading edge of future renewal in the form of increased demands on maintenance, not being aware of the big picture, tended to think of these demands as 'blips' that would soon pass. They didn't appreciate that their current renewals were mostly of smaller pre-war stocks and that, in future, they would need to cope with the large post-war expansion, which now represented 75% and more of agency portfolios. To show that those renewal requirements would never again return to anywhere near current levels, the default projections in the summary report were extended out 50 years.

When the size of the total state commitments became clear, it was easier for individual agencies to understand that this was not so much a money problem as a more serious resource challenge — where would the increased skills, equipment, and materials come from? Not from interstate, given that other states would also be coping with increased renewal demands.

These realisations were necessary to move agencies away from their traditional stance of demanding more funds and get them to start considering how to reduce future costs.

The PAC's 'big picture' message had three elements:

1. Past renewal was not a reliable guide to future requirements.
2. There was financial scope for renewal, provided some funding was switched from new to renewal.
3. There was planning time of about ten to fifteen years. Future renewal, while large, was not imminent.

New York, New York!

Selling these messages gained support from an unexpected source. New York had run into serious infrastructure funding difficulties in 1975. Nearly bankrupt, it had sought a bailout from its federal government and was initially turned down, generating the infamous *New York Daily News* headline 'Ford to City: Drop Dead!' Of course, President Gerald Ford didn't use those words, and he did eventually relent. But when the Australian media spoke of New York's problems, that message was not lost on South Australia. No one expected our Commonwealth Government to be any more generous. Indeed, Commonwealth funding for state projects was already being cut back.

New York continued to struggle for over ten years. By 1985, the city's problems were featuring in our newspapers under lurid headlines, such as 'The Worm inside the Rotten Apple' (*The Courier-Mail*, Brisbane, 24 August 1985) and 'The City that Lives in Permanent Crisis' (*The National Times*, 15–21 February 1985), accompanied by full broadsheet pages of the troubles experienced by New York.

In addition, stories started circulating privately amongst those involved with infrastructure about how bits of the Manhattan Bridge were rusting and falling into the Hudson River and how potholes in New York's cement roads had to have steel plates bolted over them because they couldn't remove the traffic long enough to repair them. In one story, these steel plates caused such havoc for the city buses that their engines were falling out. When the city sought replacements that could withstand the driving conditions, it was tentatively approached by a French company, which said it did have such a bus, but …

'But what?' it was asked.

'Well,' replied the company hesitantly, 'it's a model we normally only sell to underdeveloped countries.'

This story may be apocryphal, but the impression it made here was important because it illustrated how developed countries could revert to third-world conditions by ignoring infrastructure maintenance.

During our investigation, the committee chairman had the opportunity to go to New York. He asked me what questions I had for that city. I said, 'Just three: "When did they first realise that they had a problem?", "What did they do then?" and "What happened next?"'

The responses were heartfelt. 'We knew we had a problem when maintenance started to rise beyond our capacity.' So, what did you do? 'We stopped maintenance — we had to. We just didn't have the money.' And what happened next? 'All hell broke loose. We couldn't cope.'

We told this story in the PAC reports.

Understanding the projections

The public in 1987 was not accustomed to thinking in terms of billions of dollars. Our asset-renewal projections seemed like fantasy figures, which made it difficult to come to grips with them and easy to misconstrue them. Many saw them as forecasts or predictions and would object that 'These projections are clearly wrong! There is no way we are going to spend so much on renewal.' Then there were the comments by those who should, and probably did, know better but misconstrued for their own purposes, such as the Minister for Health, who wrote to the committee:

'The funding requirements recommended in your report are only marginally in excess of the guidelines already issued to the Commission by Treasury for future planning resources. The Commission has resolved to negotiate with the Treasury in an effort to have their guidelines marginally increased to equate with your recommended levels.' (5 April 1987, letter from the Minister for Health to the Public Accounts Commission)

Projections, of course, are not forecasts. Projections simply model what will happen if nothing changes to improve the situation. Their purpose is to show why change is needed. They do not recommend that the existing figures be financed — quite the reverse!

They also have another use. The default assumptions in our model indicated where beneficial changes could be made. For example, one of these default assumptions, necessary for the modelling, was that we would replace all the assets we currently had. But did we need to? Were our portfolios that had been designed to cope with the needs of the rapidly growing 1950s and 1960s still relevant in the late 1980s? This was unlikely and needed to be re-examined. Indeed, studies had already shown large-scale under-utilisation in schools. Then, in 1983, the *Report of the Enquiry into Health Services in South Australia* by Professor Sydney Sax (the Sax Enquiry) argued for a 30% reduction in the health sector. Resistance to this reduction might have inspired the Minister for Health's artful interpretation of our study.

Other default assumptions, such as no change in maintenance or renewal practices, or in technology, also suggested directions for cost reduction.

Misinterpretation

The most significant misinterpretation, however, was not to recognise that the projections were designed for, and only suitable for, financial and resource-planning purposes, not for physical intervention.

This misinterpretation continues today. Projections are based on 'average economic lives', using the law of large numbers. The economic life of a specific pipe, sewer, piece of plant, or stretch of road, etc., will vary around the average, and the range can be quite broad. When we project renewal for many similar components (say, all hospital generators), we can reasonably expect that, to a certain extent, 'overs' will cancel out 'unders', and provide a generally reliable financial projection.

But the 'law of large numbers' applies only where we actually have large numbers!

This means they cannot be applied to an individual component for physical intervention. The mathematical law of large numbers doesn't change, no matter how much extra engineering detail is added to the models. Despite this, many detailed engineering projections were developed based on the renewal-costing paradigm of the PAC and are still used, claiming to project the renewal timing of individual components, and used to program physical intervention.

References such as 'These assets have exceeded their economic life, thus must be immediately replaced' indicate this misinterpretation has occurred, for the nature of an average is that there will be some assets that last shorter times (and may have now been removed and replaced) and those that last longer. After all, this is how we get our average! At best, such projections may be used as an indication that further examination is due.

So, while asset managers today may roll their eyes at the story of the minister in Holland who was not interested in the general probability of dyke failure but insisted on knowing 'which dyke and when?', they make the same mistake whenever they base asset intervention of any particular asset or component on 'average' economic life.

A strategic plan

The PAC examined the maintenance, renewal, planning, and accounting practices in each agency, and its summary report used this information to suggest, with examples, ideas for agency management and public reporting in what was the first general set of AM guidelines for application to varied government infrastructure portfolios.

The first committee requirement was for all agencies to prepare a strategic plan. It stressed: 'Strategic plans do not have to be complex. Indeed, they may be nothing more than a statement of the most important changes that have to occur, with some indication of how and by when things will happen.' It argued this was incumbent on both central and individual agencies.

Improved parliamentary information

The committee considered parliament's need for improved asset information as urgent (i.e., to be provided in the next financial year). This was to include the non-cash costs or 'annual consumption' of assets. All proposals for new capital works were to include non-cash costs and should provide information on the organisation's total asset holdings, growth history, the returns (cash and non-cash) delivered by the agency's total portfolio, and the change expected from the project proposal.

The committee argued that these reports to parliament should be in accrual terms, with balance sheets provided, and that current asset values should be used rather than out-of-date and irrelevant historical costs. It pointed out: 'If taxes, or charges, are set too low because the real costs of capital maintenance have been under-valued (or ignored), then future generations will have to pay more than their fair share to restore the capital infrastructure'.

Since a stumbling block to moving to accrual accounting could be valuing assets, it set out a nine-step roadmap to developing the necessary valuations, using as a starting point the figures already provided in the final report (53rd PAC Report, p. 39).

However, only partial improvements were made.

Attitude change

It was clear that there would be little benefit from having planning time unless this time was used to make changes, and the needed changes would be difficult.

It had long been the practice of not only agencies but also governments to allocate maintenance and renewal resources largely based on what was allocated the previous year, plus or minus a bit, depending on how flush with funds they were. But if resources were to be efficiently allocated, they needed to be determined by future renewal requirements, not past allocations. Funds would therefore have to be withdrawn from some areas and allocated to others, both within agencies and between agencies.

To illustrate the significance of this reallocation problem, the final report, i.e. the summary, presented pie charts that showed renewal requirements in the different five-year periods. Transport renewal represented about 16% of total renewal requirements from 1981 to 1985 but only 7% some ten years later. Highways renewal represented only 14% of the total in 1981–85 but rose to 28% of the renewal total in the following ten years. Changing allocations of this order is politically difficult but necessary — hence the necessity for a change of attitude to allocate according to total community needs rather than specific agency wants. All agencies and ministers needed to understand and act on this. Not an easy task! Nor, in the event, was it undertaken. The problems continued.

It seems odd now, but initially, many thought that buildings and other structures would 'last forever'. After all, they looked pretty solid. Until the PAC started looking into the renewal of individual components to extend the life of the whole, the focus had been on construction rather than reconstruction.

This change in focus to reconstruction was perhaps the main contribution of the committee for, whereas it had previously been little considered, now it began to be measured and managed.

So how was this major project, the first research exercise by the PAC, received by individual agencies, government bodies, the media, and the public? The reactions are what we look at in the next chapter.

CHAPTER 7

REACTIONS

Agencies

The parliamentary PAC was accountable to the South Australian Parliament and needed to inform it first. The agencies didn't get to see the result of our analysis until after it had been tabled in the House. This came as a bit of a shock to all of them as they were not used to looking at their asset portfolios in the way that we were doing, and agency reactions were initially concerned, alarmed — and negative.

This led to some amusing correspondence as agencies came to terms with the substance of the reports. For one agency, we had demonstrated that, while it claimed it put maintenance first, it actually focused primarily on new and major reconstruction, as evident from its organisational structure and annual reports. The first response of this agency was, 'Penny's got it all wrong, and we are going to have a word with the minister.' By that afternoon, this had been amended to 'Penny's still got it all wrong, but we are not speaking with the minister.' By the following morning, it was, 'Well, it's not all wrong!' And by the time we produced the final summary report some months later, they were in complete agreement with our findings. As, indeed, were all agencies, even Housing. It was a record for the PAC: eight reports and complete agreement! Never been known before.

Media

The reports didn't make much of a dent on the media. The final media presentation attracted three TV channels and sundry press, but the questions were inane. At its close, I found the reporter from the local newspaper, a young woman, wandering around the basement of Parliament House, looking lost and trying to find her way out. As I helped her, she turned a bewildered face to me and, in hushed and awed tones, said, referring to the PAC Chairman's address, 'He was talking billions! I don't understand billions.' So much for intelligent press coverage.

Central agencies and the university

While explaining the future renewal problems of the Royal Adelaide Hospital to one of the deputies in the Auditor-General's Office who was on the hospital's board, I was dismayed at his response. Showing great anxiety, he exclaimed, 'My goodness, we can't let the board see this!' Avoiding information that could be a problem was, unfortunately, not an uncommon response.

However, not all saw the large renewal figures as a cause for dismay and anxiety. In the city, shortly after our figures were released, I was greeted by the Under Treasurer, who braved the city traffic to dash across the road to tell me enthusiastically that our figures had helped the state retain its triple-A credit rating. The rating agencies had seen the renewal figures as an indication of the state's wealth and not its mounting future debt!

Still others had the foresight to see difficulties I had not envisaged. Just after starting the work with the PAC, I attended the University of Adelaide's Economics Department Christmas party and, naturally, I told my former colleagues about the work we were doing. One of them turned pale with anxiety and said that it wasn't only infrastructure renewal that was unfunded, neither was the university's superannuation fund! Now, he realised, this had to compete with the government's unfunded infrastructure renewal, and he was concerned. (He would have been even more concerned had he realised that the state's long-service leave commitments were also unfunded!)

Parliament and government

The parliament established a sub-committee to report to it on asset management. The government, meanwhile, had set up a task force to review the work of the PAC. The original intention of this task force, I discovered from one of its members, had been to rubbish the report and undermine belief in it, but as it became evident that its results would not reflect poorly on the current administration, as had been expected, but instead reflected the results of numerous past administrations, they were more inclined to treat it seriously and ended up reinforcing all our results.

The PAC members themselves

During the almost two-and-a-half years I was with them, the committee members became increasingly interested in economics and began using economic concepts in their own work. There was one inquiry into a port authority that had invested in a computer system some seven years previously but had yet to have any output from it. One of the committee members cut into the numerous excuses presented to demand, 'What is the opportunity cost of that?' Shortly afterwards, I noticed the committee secretary pass him a note. It read: 'You have pleasantly surprised our resident economist!'

So many of my board presentations consisted of explaining economics that, on one occasion towards the end, the chairman leant back in his chair and said, 'And what kind of an economics degree do we get out of this?' and when I murmured something about an honorary degree, he exploded, 'Honorary, be damned. We've worked hard for this!' And they had.

Their interest in economics then extended to other work that I was doing. At one stage, I had explained to them how the multiplier concept was being misused and how consultants' claims such as, 'The Festival of Arts returns $7.53 for every dollar of government support' were utter nonsense. They said I should write a letter to the editor, and I was disappointed. Miserably, I said to the PAC secretary, 'I thought they understood.' He replied, 'They did! They want you to write it where politicians will read it!' — which showed how little I still understood about politics.

The multiplier conversation was apropos of a book that I was co-writing and editing, looking into the impact of the first Australian Grand Prix, which was held in Adelaide in 1985. The idea for this had arisen over coffee with Paul Van der Lee, my former section leader at the water authority, who was then heading up marketing for the Department of Tourism. We knew we wanted the Grand Prix to be a success but were worried that if it were, it could spark many worthless 'public events' because the government had no idea how to evaluate their likely success.

There had been no study of the costs and benefits of a Grand Prix anywhere in the world, yet its value was always being touted. We decided to do such a study and publish it to coincide with the second Grand Prix in 1986. I asked the then Premier of South Australia, John Bannon, whom I had known since university, to launch it. I was sure that he would like to do that, for he had secured the last election with a record majority and was in no doubt that the success of the Grand Prix was in large measure responsible for the size of his win.

Naturally, I had also invited the PAC committee members to the launch. When the premier walked into the room and saw them all, he thought they were planning to investigate the Grand Prix, and he turned pale! Fortunately, the chairman — quick to recognise what he was thinking — took him aside and explained the relationship.

A few years later, when the state government was being urged by some to secure the Commonwealth Games for Adelaide, arguing that if it did, 'we would get lots of new sporting venues', several of our committee members from both sides of the House objected, as they now understood the ongoing costs of such infrastructure. I was proud of them for that.

Infrastructure agencies across Australia

The water industry had already enthusiastically adopted the idea of asset management long before we produced the final PAC report, and it was busy spreading the word to its colleagues interstate and overseas. The generic nature of our investigation of seven separate agencies had also made it attractive to other states, for they could see that they were likely to experience the same issues for the same reasons.

An idea whose time had come

The PAC reports were not the only infrastructure reports to be produced around 1987, but they were the only ones that dealt with asset management.

In April 1986, the UK Institution of Civil Engineers produced the *Second Report of the Infrastructure Planning Group*, a detailed study into UK demand for assets over the coming years. It was a fact-finding exercise for politicians to use in planning future infrastructure acquisition. It did not look at renewing ageing assets, as such, nor at infrastructure management.

In the USA in 1987, the National Council on Public Works Improvement produced its *Executive Summaries of Nine Studies*, and in 1988, a much larger volume, *Fragile Foundations: A Report on America's Public Works*. The latter was a major report that looked at how much it would cost to not only replace all of America's ageing assets but also bring them up to the latest standards, plus fill in the gaps where infrastructure had not yet been provided for all. So, it included renewal, expansion, and upgrade, but with insufficient detail to enable these elements to be identified and managed separately.

The aim was to make the figure as large as possible to convince politicians to take the matter seriously. (Later, I was to meet with one of the authors of this report, an MP, and when I talked about how we might improve infrastructure decision-making, she reacted negatively, 'If we can't get the capital projects we want, it wouldn't be worth going into politics!')

America, as a rich country, was used to dealing with problems by throwing money at them, so its focus on the costs alone probably made sense to it. Australia, on the other hand, had no such illusions. We didn't expect money to be easily forthcoming and knew that we would need to present a well-documented case if this were to happen. We also knew priorities would need to be set, so our focus was on management.

The UK and the USA studies covered much larger populations and were far wider in scope than the South Australian study, which covered a population of two million people and had a restricted focus on asset renewal for a mere seven agencies. Our study might be considered insignificant. However, it was precisely our restricted focus that allowed us to go into depth and develop workable asset management processes and practices.

Public presentations

The practical management focus of the PAC reports made them easy to convey asset management messages to our varied audiences.

When the final report was released, there was a flurry of speaking requests, but the first two presentations I delivered had the most interesting responses. In November 1986, I delivered a short address to the World Housing Congress, which alerted the CSIRO to the work we were doing. In February 1987, I delivered a presentation to the National Accountants in Government Conference in Perth. The latter was a full presentation, and it was tricky as the results of the last four reports had yet to be presented to parliament, so I could not use them. I chose to illustrate the main issues, using roads as the simplest way to get across the notion that our current renewal expenditures were not a good indication of our future needs, and why.

I worked on that one paper every day for six weeks! My session was the last one. After listening to the other presenters at the conference and marvelling at their beautifully produced slides, I knew that, despite my weeks of effort, my presentation would be the least professional heard that day. It was thus a blessing that I had the smallest room with the smallest audience. There were about 110 people, but given the over 2,000 attendees at the conference, you could say that asset management then was a 'boutique' interest. Most had come out of curiosity.

At the end of the presentation, however, a strange thing happened. Instead of rapidly exiting and heading for the bar, as usually happens after the last session of the day, the audience stayed, and question time ran for well over an hour! The audience might have been small, but it was enthusiastic.

At the end, someone asked, 'Surely, with all the technological advances we have made, we should be able to design all our buildings to last for 200 or 300 years.' And I, having dealt with the problem of physical lives that already greatly exceeded their functional or economic lives, replied in genuine astonishment, 'My goodness, why would we want to?' That caused the chairman to bring the session to a halt.

That conference paper was subsequently reproduced in *The Public Sector: Contemporary Readings in Accounting and Auditing*, edited by Guthrie, Parker and Shand (1990), which led to me often being referred to in accounting papers. My favourite all-time citation was, 'Accountants don't know how to handle this, but Dr Penny Burns says …', which occurred in one accounting society's practice papers.

Incidentally, when I presented to the same accounting conference six years later, I had the plenary hall and over two-thirds of the attendees. A lot had happened in those six years, and asset management was no longer a 'boutique interest'. In the following chapters, I will trace the developments that helped this to happen.

On a subsequent visit to Perth, the Highways Deputy Commissioner told me enthusiastically that he loved my paper (maybe because of the focus on roads) and had restructured his corporate planning branch based on it! I don't know how he did that, but I was pleased to think my six weeks of effort had not been in vain.

My reactions

If the accountants had a strong reaction to my paper, it was nothing compared to my reaction to them. An audience of 110 might be small by their association's standards, but it was huge by mine. I was not new to public speaking. As a PhD student, I had, for the past five years, presented at both economics and agricultural economics conferences every year. But experimental economics, my topic, was as new to those audiences as asset management was to this one. Today it is a recognised category of economics, but at that time it was considered an impossibility. So numbers were small. They could be as low as five. There would be me and my mate who turned up in support, the other speaker and his mate, and the chairman. But no matter how small, you gave it your all. That had been my speaking experience until asset management — and then everything changed!

The other thing that changed was the venue. In my university years, the presentation space was a lecture theatre, and my conference accommodation was usually a student hostel: a single bed, a desk, a lamp, a cupboard, and a wastepaper basket, lino on the floor with the odd dead cockroach in the corner, communal bathrooms — basic! I was completely unprepared for the luxury of the Perth Sheraton.

At the gala dinner for that conference, I was gratified to be invited to join the table of 'The Untouchables' — that is, the table allocated to the auditors-general — and I got to know them all. This was to be very helpful later when I was presenting at accounting conferences, introducing asset management and valuation principles, and arguing the case for accrual accounting and for replacement values over historical costs.

It puzzled me why the auditors-general could understand and agree with the points I was making about accrual accounting and yet not adopt them. That is until they explained they could only audit according to generally accepted policies and practices (GAPP).

It continues to be a source of frustration for me that those who are in the best position to see what is going wrong with these generally accepted policies and practices seem to be the least able to do anything about them!

CHAPTER 8

MOVING ON — MY STORY

Again, it was time to move on. As much as I had not wanted to leave the EWS, I was even more reluctant to leave the PAC, which had been so much fun. But my work there was done, and I had decided where to go next over a year before.

As the end of the first year of my secondment to the PAC came up, the PAC Secretary had shown me a job advertised by the Public Buildings Department. The job specification required someone to 'remove all fluctuations in the South Australian construction industry'! I protested that Public Buildings could not do this, whomever it employed. It might build a large proportion of schools and office buildings, but the demand decisions were made elsewhere. Even these represented only about a third or less of state-funded construction, and the department had little, if any, influence over local or federal construction expenditure in the state and none over private construction. I declared it a non-job!

These jobs were not as rare as they should have been. They were mainly designed to boost the number of people reporting to top executives and thus make them feel more important. I was surprised that the PAC Secretary had not recognised this for himself. But, of course, he had. He had also seen something that I had not. With a happy smile, he replied, 'Exactly! You can make this job anything you like!'

I won the job, and as the PAC one-year secondment stretched out to close to two-and-a-half years and we saw more and more asset management issues needing attention, it was obvious what I wanted my next job to be.

Finishing with the PAC

I officially started with Public Buildings, now re-named Housing and Construction, on 1 April, 1987, an auspicious day, but there were still two more agency reports to be tabled, and the whole of the final summary report had yet to be written. I split my time between the two agencies, but even so, it would not have been possible without the willing cooperation of the other two researchers. They not only put aside their own projects to get this finished but also gave up their weekends to enable us to table the last two agency reports.

Then, with just the summary report to go, the House decided to rise early for Easter. We now had less than a week to finish! So, again, it was all hands on deck and, at one stage, even the chairman rang and asked, 'Do you need another hand on a pencil?' He then came in about nine that evening and wrote the section we had talked about a year before on the untying of federal government grants to the states. It is very rare for PAC chairmen to do any writing in their reports, and I was grateful for his help at this critical time.

The final report that would go on to have so much of an impact on asset management was written in just 54 hours from go to woe, including two presentations to the committee! But, of course, its actual preparation time was almost two and a half years, not including the original work for the water authority.

That final summary report was tabled on 15 April, and now there remained just one task — to present this work to the Biennial PAC Conference in Sydney in six weeks. If the state PAC committees and the auditors-general, who usually all attended, saw value in our work, there was a chance that asset management could be taken up Australia-wide, and I was very hopeful. I was also keen to be 'in at the kill' in Sydney, as it were, but I was no longer on the PAC staff. While they kindly offered to include me in their official party, I needed my new department to pay my costs and give me the time.

And here, we struck a bit of a problem. Well, two problems. Having had to wait for me for about fifteen months, my new director was not well inclined to support the PAC any further. Also, my new position, having not been planned for interstate travel, had a travel budget of just a few hundred dollars. So, a bit of a challenge.

Getting to Melbourne and Sydney

I had received a request to address the CSIRO in Melbourne. Lex Blaikie, Head of the Building Division, and Professor Frank Bromilow, Head of the Architecture Department at the University of Melbourne and advisor to the CSIRO, had read my presentation to the World Housing Congress in November and were interested to know more.

Even before the PAC took up the asset management work, Lex Blaikie's division had been very active in this area through its publication *Infact*. The division had been attempting to model needed maintenance but didn't have the information access that the PAC did. It had a small selection of schools but could only access figures on maintenance actually carried out. There was no way of telling whether that maintenance was enough, excessive, or indeed spent in the right areas. This frustrated the division, so it was delighted with the PAC's work and keen to speak with me.

I arranged to meet with them just before the Sydney PAC conference, so that now, with the Adelaide–Melbourne return airfare taken care of by the CSIRO, my travel budget was just enough to get me the rest of the way plus a couple of nights of cheap accommodation, so that solved one of my problems. It didn't solve everything, though, for while the CSIRO had written requesting my attendance in Melbourne, I still needed an excuse for Sydney — an excuse that my new director could not refuse.

As I stared out of my new office windows at the grey April skies, I thought about how much they matched the greyness of my chances. Then, and I have no idea where this inspiration came from, probably desperation,

I picked up the phone and rang the Director of Public Works in Sydney, announcing myself as Dr Penny Burns (PhDs were not so common then, and certainly not for females). I explained to the secretary that I had just finished a two-and-a-half-year study with the PAC looking at the cost and timing of renewing all of South Australia's infrastructure, and I thought the director might be interested in the results. She thought so, too, and put me through.

An hour's conversation later, it turned out he was very interested, so I said I would be in Sydney in May and asked if he would like me to speak with his executive panel. Yes, he would and would write a letter of request to my department. Then, thinking that these guys probably talked to each other, and I didn't want to get offside with anyone, I did the same for the Department of Public Works in Melbourne, with the same results.

Looking back, I now consider it one of life's miracles that both directors were free to take my call that afternoon, and their secretaries were willing to put me through. It is yet another example of the luck that followed this project.

So pleased was I to have solved my Sydney PAC biennial conference problem that I was slow to realise that I had done it yet again — been so task-focused that I had not considered the consequences. If I had thought much about it, and honestly, I hadn't thought at all, I imagined my director would be proud that his officer had been invited to speak by the two largest public works authorities in the country. He wasn't.

Fortunately, the CEO was.

New opportunities arise

In Melbourne at the CSIRO, I was introduced to Charles Johnson, who was busy designing the brochure for the upcoming Canberra National Infrastructure Forum. In the heading was the phrase 'infrastructure needs'. I took issue with Charles about this, saying that since we didn't know what we had nor what we wanted, 'needs' was hardly the right word. He protested that he had spent all morning getting it in. I suggested he take all afternoon and get it out again! We had a spirited but good-natured conversation, the result of which was that the CSIRO arranged a speaking slot for me at the forum, which was to prove instrumental in what was to happen next.

The next day, on my way to meet with Victorian Department of Public Works, I got caught in a drenching rainstorm and arrived, soaking wet and dishevelled, only to be told that the CEO, with whom I had spoken, was home with a cold. I was left to introduce myself. As I looked around the room, something seemed off. I said, 'You don't know why I am here, do you?' Someone said, 'No, the boss just said to come, and it would be interesting.'

'It will, and if someone can find me a hot coffee and a place to dry my jacket, I will happily tell you.' That was my unimpressive, but nevertheless memorable, introduction to a group I was to become very friendly with, and work with many times over the following twenty years.

The Sydney Public Works meeting was not so fraught, but it also produced long-lasting contacts and led to my involvement in writing the first state asset management manual.

At last, it was time for the address of the PAC Chairman, John Klunder, to the PAC conference, which I was greatly looking forward to, but his session chairman was so taken by the fact that I had the same given name as his daughter that the idiot wasted a good fifteen to twenty minutes talking enthusiastically about me! At first, I was amused, then embarrassed, and finally distressed that John had so little time to talk about our work. He took it more calmly than I did.

Fortunately, Chris Jay, the well-respected senior reporter for the Australian Financial Review, was called upon to comment. This was the same Chris Jay who had spoken at the last biennial PAC conference in Adelaide just before we started our work. He had been given a full copy of John's paper. After clarifying that we were indeed quoting prices in 1985 dollars and not guessing at future inflation, he said how tremendously impressed he was with what we had done and how important it was that everyone should know about it. With this endorsement, by the time the delegates went on the end-of-session harbour cruise, all knew who I was, and many wanted to talk about asset management.

So, in just six weeks, changing the focus of my new role as Manager, Policy Development from 'controlling construction fluctuations' to 'asset management' was already beginning to take shape with the opportunity to influence not just South Australia but the whole of Australia. Importantly, I now had my next two questions:

- How can the PAC recommendations be implemented?
- How to appeal to architects and other related disciplines?

PART THREE: IMPLEMENTATION

APRIL 1987– AUGUST 1989

THE DEPARTMENT OF CONSTRUCTION

The third part of this volume describes my new role as Manager, Policy Development for the Public Buildings Department, where I looked at ways to implement the Public Accounts Committee's asset management recommendations in my department and influence other related disciplines. After my appointment, the Public Buildings Department was renamed the Department of Construction (which indicates the mindset I needed to work with). The dominant professionals in this department were the architects, so that is where I needed to start.

CHAPTER 9

NOT EVERYTHING WORKS THE FIRST TIME

Here is what I tried in searching for an answer to:

Q 5: HOW CAN THE PAC RECOMMEN- DATIONS BE IMPLEMENTED?

Public works

After working for the EWS and the PAC, both high-profile organisations, it was a shock to find myself now in a demoralised department. The Department of Construction was losing work to the private sector and facing criticism from all quarters. It was desperately looking for a new role. My own newly-created position of 'Industry Policy Advisor', designed to elevate the department by 'advising' the construction industry at large, was evidence of this. We were scarcely able to advise ourselves, let alone others.

South Australia was not alone in this situation. All public works departments across the country were experiencing the same pressure, except for NSW under the innovative leadership of Premier Greiner, who was charting his own path. The prevailing view seemed to be that the private sector could do everything more efficiently because it had a 'profit motive'. Without this as a spur, it was considered that staff would be lazy, incompetent, and inefficient.

This view was supported by state treasuries struggling to cope with reduced funding from the federal government. They were looking for ways to cut costs, and 'outsourcing' to the private sector was promoted as a way of being more efficient. Many articles claimed that outsourcing could reduce costs by as much as 20%. It was assumed that this was because of the much-publicised public service 'inefficiency', and when savings did result, this was seen as confirmation.

Initially, it went unnoticed that most of the savings arose not so much from greater efficiency but from work not being done. If, for example, a window-cleaning contract let to a cleaning company resulted in the windows being cleaned less often, this was considered efficiency. However, only costs were measured. Service decline was too difficult to measure, and so was assumed not to happen.

Two sources of 'savings' had serious consequences. In the days of 'stewardship' (before the mid-1980s), construction was designed to last. It could be said (and was said) that it was 'over-engineered'. Initially, the robust nature of construction meant it was possible to neglect a certain amount of routine maintenance and still have a functioning asset, and this yielded an early source of 'savings'.

Such maintenance deferrals, of course, had limitations, but in the excitement of the new, no one was looking! However, as more and more construction in subsequent years was left to the private sector, motivated by profits rather than asset longevity, it failed to be recognised that the level of maintenance now needed to be increased to compensate for less robust construction.

Instead, service declined — but so gradually that it was not noticed.

'Savings' were also achieved by removing the public sector commitment to training and apprenticeship. Again, the consequences were ignored at first. By the time they were recognised, the shift to the private sector was well advanced.

Early recognition by local government

Asset management was introduced at the state government level via the PAC's reports and recommendations; however, it was quickly taken up by practitioners, operators, and maintainers in local government, who were daily witnesses to asset deterioration and wanted to do something about it.

Leading the field was Roger Byrne, an engineer with GHD (Gutteridge, Haskins and Davies) in Melbourne, Victoria. Many engineering asset managers working in water and sewerage and local government in the early 1990s and 2000s and, equally, many local government administrators would credit Roger with being their introduction to asset management. He was exceptional. What made him stand out was his recognition that technical knowledge alone was insufficient; asset management also required an understanding of economics and accounting. Whenever he learnt something new, he would write it up as a 'briefing note' for his GHD clients. Later these briefing notes became the basis for the *National Asset Management Manual for Local Government 1994,* the first local government asset management manual, and the basis for what was later to become the world-renowned IIMM (*International Infrastructure Management Manual*).

Meanwhile, back in Adelaide, figuring that asset management, like charity, needed to begin at home, I looked to how it could be implemented in the Department of Construction. Although looking for a new role, the department was still to be convinced that asset management was it. Many, particularly the architects, who were the dominant profession, clung to the hope that they could continue with construction rather than reconstruction and renewal, and were rejoicing in their newly chosen construction-focused logo, 'SACON' (South Australian Construction).

Life-cycle renewal forecasting

Would the move to asset management be helped by the department developing new knowledge, competencies, and attitudes? This is what I decided to explore, and an opportunity to do it arose very early. On my second day with the Department of Construction, I arrived to find two fellow branch managers waiting for me with a proposition. One had a job that was over time and budget, and the department's major client, the Education Department, was not pleased. The proposal was for me to finish the job (at no additional cost to the project!) in such a way that the client would think the delay was worth it. The other branch manager suggested it would also be good if I could perform this miracle whilst finding a use for a troublesome regional manager who needed to be relocated. I was amused to note that they offered me nothing in return for taking on these tasks, and I did wonder whether I was being set up to fail. Nevertheless, it seemed a fun and worthwhile challenge, so I agreed.

The Education Department staff wanted information to inform their planning of the maintenance budget. Construction had interpreted this request as a need for detailed condition assessments and had started on a room-by-room, component-by-component assessment — for hundreds of schools! No wonder they were over time and budget, and the job was nowhere near finished. Education only wanted a money estimate, not details of all the physical jobs that could be done. This was an opportunity to apply the PAC life-cycle renewal forecasting model. The job was completed, and the client was delighted that he now had a method he could reuse.

Are you spending fast enough?

This success led me to think that I could indeed encourage the adoption of asset management. However, such optimism received a blow when I attended my first — and last — budget meeting. The only question at that meeting was how fast we could spend our budget, not how well we could spend it. Both the Treasury and the South Australian Parliament were complaining we were not spending fast enough. No one wanted to take the time to consider how to spend more wisely. With this pressure on the department, how was I to argue for better asset decision-making?

Thinking on this, I could see that asset management needed to go hand in hand with change management — and that we needed to operate on many fronts.

Zero-based replacement (ZBR)

Obviously, reducing cost and wastage was not going to be enough. I tried a new approach, which I called 'zero-based replacement'. Normal practice was to replace anything that failed without considering whether it was still needed. I argued that renewal should face the same critical analysis as a new project. My director liked the ZBR idea, which had the potential to demonstrate that the department could 'add value' as well as reduce some of the backlog maintenance that the Treasury had been agitating about. He was keen for his staff to develop ideas for alternatives to replacement 'as is' and, for almost nine months, various groups met to think about this — and got nowhere! They were construction-oriented architects and engineers, chosen for 'doing' rather than 'decision-making'. The pressure to do things quickly, as the budget meeting had shown, meant they had developed necessary techniques, such as not thinking too long or too slowly about alternatives. Replacement 'as is' was quickest. Searching for alternatives was not only beyond their skill set but contrary to the felt needs of the department.

I decided to demonstrate what could be done. Looking through a list of maintenance items, I noticed one for the replacement of a school boiler that had broken down some eighteen months before. Sympathetically, I said to the Maintenance Supervisor, 'You must have had a lot of complaints about that one. Last winter was the worst we have had in many years.' His answer rocked me. 'No, not a one!'

Curious, I contacted the school. What problems had they experienced over the past eighteen months because of the failure of the boiler? None, really, was the answer. 'Our problems are not in the winter but in the summertime. On hot days, we have to crowd everyone into the library, which is the only air-conditioned room we have. We really could do with air conditioning.'

Thinking this an opportunity to do some creative zero-based renewal thinking, I gathered a small group consisting of an architect, a surveyor, an engineer, and the maintenance supervisor and suggested to them that instead of replacing the boiler, which the school did not appear to want, we consider what options we had. We took a tour of the school and spoke to the staff. The surveyor noted a stand of trees to the side of the building that minimised the winter chills, whilst the engineer quickly noted that the main reason everyone was feeling so hot and stuffy in the classrooms was that all the windows were kept shut ('for safety reasons'), so there was no ventilation. The architect suggested a few simple modifications to retain safety but increase ventilation. This would, he said, account for most of the classrooms, but the few that would receive the brunt of the summer sun could be shaded and would also benefit from air conditioning.

If we used our maintenance resources to do this, instead of replacing the boiler, the school's working environment would be greatly improved and the children and staff much happier. I considered it a good illustration that asset management was more than just maintenance.

Sadly, this is not the end of the story.

Ideas are one thing, people are another!

Feeling pleased with the creative contributions of the team, I wrote up a short report and asked my assistant if he wouldn't mind taking a few photographs of the school and boiler to illustrate the problem we had so effectively tackled.

Thirty minutes later, I had a phone call from him saying it wasn't there. 'What do you mean it's not there? A school can't just disappear!'

'No, not the school; the boiler isn't here. The school tells me that the maintenance supervisor has removed it because the replacement is coming tomorrow!'

This was the same maintenance supervisor who had been part of our team analysing the zero-based renewal problem over the past few weeks! I was floored.

I called him in and asked him what on earth he was doing. We knew the boiler was not needed, and the maintenance resources could be used more effectively for the school.

'Oh,' he said, 'I thought that was just an academic exercise!'

Change takes time! And considerable patience.

Data items do not constitute knowledge

The PAC had asked a range of new questions, and seeking answers to these questions had greatly expanded the range of data collected. Seeing this, many sought to add more data items to their own asset registers whilst happily chanting 'knowledge is power'. It went unrecognised that knowledge resulted from the selection and analysis of the data. That is what yielded the power of the committee's results, not simply more data.

SACON's database was the envy of all public works departments simply because it was the biggest. We could identify no fewer than 26 different types of school toilet blocks! No one could say why this was an advantage other than that data were good, so more data must be better!

But was it? Already it was hard to keep it up to date. Errors were occurring, and users were not trusting the data. On sunny days, our architects would choose to ignore the database, claiming it to be unreliable and making it a reason for visiting the site, an exercise that the database was designed to render unnecessary. Also, the education facility managers would point to a school on the database that they knew had burned down months before and ask how it came to be still on our database.

We needed to cull. Again, I gathered a small team, this one consisting of an architect, a planner, and an engineer, with me as the economist, and we agreed that if none of us, from our different perspectives, could think of a use for any data item, we would simply eliminate it.

Pen in one hand, ruler in the other, I faced my small advisory panel. We had only gone down about eight lines before we came to such an item. 'Good,' I said and positioned the ruler. But now that it was a reality and not simply an academic position, alarm caused them to freeze. Fear of making a wrong decision prevented any decision — and the database continued to grow.

Part of the problem was that those responsible for managing the database were not those who used it. Later I found this to be a common problem in asset management. Not knowing how it would be used, we were at risk of collecting the wrong data, or data at an inappropriate level of aggregation or timeliness. Moreover, what few realised at the time — and perhaps even now — is that data, by itself, are useless. Without the processes and institutions to take that data and transform it into something useful, we might as well not have it.

For example, if we could record utilisation, we thought we could move accommodation from surplus to deficit areas. Yet the administration had no process for this relocation. As a result, no department with surplus accommodation would admit it for fear that it could not get it back if needed later. Meanwhile, any department the minister approved for new accommodation wanted custom-designed accommodation, not some other department's 'cast offs'.

Whilst asset management has resulted in many improvements, the transformation of data into information and then into knowledge (i.e. usable information) still has far to go.

Otis Elevator Company

I had been struggling to get the department to believe that asset management was the way forward. My director was keen, but the other directors were not. However, the time came when they were going on a two-day retreat to set directions for the department, and my director asked for something he could present that would capture their imaginations and allow us to adopt asset management as a role of the department. Knowing the aversion of the other directors, I wrote a paper with no reference to asset management, and I left my name off the paper. I titled the presentation 'The value of information to the future of SACON' and told them the following story about the Otis Elevator Company.

Otis built and serviced elevators. Its large-volume business had been built on the premise of shaving the once-off construction price and recouping through ongoing service contracts. But now Otis had a problem. Its initial captive service market was in danger of disappearing. A large geographic distribution combined with a non-uniform standard of service had encouraged the development of smaller, localised service firms, many of them staffed by ex-Otis employees. They were able to provide quicker and cheaper service. How did Otis react?

Otis took two actions. One, it improved the training given to service staff and staffed its telephone-line centres with highly trained operators to record the problems they received. Two, it used this information base to create a competitive advantage.

Firstly, it capitalised on its extensive geographic distribution to record and analyse service problems nationally. Then it installed diagnostic equipment in its lifts, which fed information directly into the centralised record system. Combined with maintenance and system records, this enabled Otis to predict problems and carry out corrective services while attending to routine maintenance.

The combination of information and training enabled Otis to lower the unit cost of service, develop preventative measures, and regain its competitive edge. Otis realised that information linked to operational activities is a source of value that customers are prepared to pay for because they didn't really want a cheaper way to fix malfunctioning elevators — they wanted the elevator not to fail in the first place.

Focusing on the customer's need rather than their own input won the day!

The paper went on to show how SACON could use its own extensive information to improve its standing, and you can read the whole paper on the Talking Infrastructure website at www.talkinginfrastructure.com/tams.

On the Monday after the retreat, my director was able to announce success! However, what followed reminded me of the wisdom of the adage 'be careful what you wish for'.

We should be the state's asset manager!

Naturally, I also shared this story with my friends in other Australian construction and public works departments, and it was not long before they were all writing to me exclaiming excitedly, 'We should be the state's asset manager.' This was, of course, not the message to be extracted from the Otis story. It wasn't that Otis got to choose what to do, but rather that its ability to know what was needed was why elevator owners got to choose Otis.

My fault! I should have made it much clearer.

The reason for Otis's success is that it thought of what it was doing from the customer's perspective. Rather than focusing on its own needs, it focused on what was important to its customers — that the elevator remained in service with no unexpected outages. It then developed a product (its diagnostics) to ensure provisions of this service. It was not Otis deciding what to do, but Otis recognising how it could be of service.

I had to explain to my friends that they could not be their state's asset manager because they only saw one side of the picture. They understood the assets, but they were not in a position to understand either the demand for those assets or the issues connected with the related resources (information, budgets, labour, political pressures) that government agencies such as education, health, prisons, indeed all other budget-dependent agencies, had to manage.

I said if you took your car to a mechanic and he reported that the engine was shot and needed replacement, you wouldn't automatically agree.

Instead, you might gasp at the cost and immediately start thinking of options — perhaps catching the bus, getting a new car, or hoping that you might get that promotion and, with it, a company car. Then there would be all the other demands on your money at the time. None of these things the mechanic can know. He only knows the state of the engine. He can advise; he cannot decide. Public works, I said, is in the position of the mechanic. It knows some things but not all things. It can advise but not decide.

No one simple solution to maintenance decisions

At this time, many process changes for managing maintenance were being considered. For example, it had been suggested that money for school maintenance could be given to the principal, who would know the school's needs better than most. Then there was the story of the headmaster who had declared that if he were to get his hands on the maintenance money, he would spend it all on trees. Stories such as these naturally caused concern among the maintenance fraternity.

Other suggestions included establishing a general 'maintenance charge' within which public works would determine and carry out the work needed. But who was to determine the need? There was no clear winner amongst the ideas submitted, but agencies and treasuries would continue to experiment, information would be gathered, and new approaches considered. This was asset management in practice, an ever-changing process of learning.

CHAPTER 10

MAKING CHANGE, SLOWLY

Selling an idea to someone who sees it as a clear advantage is not a difficult task. The engineers in the water authority came to see it that way, and so did the members of the PAC and, eventually, all the infrastructure agencies involved in the study. As the architects were the dominant professionals in my new department, this raised the question:

Q 6: HOW DO WE APPEAL TO ARCHITECTS, AUDIT AND OTHER DISCIPLINES?

Our architects were looking for something that would give them an edge and, in effect, raise their profile in the public service. But would they see asset management in that light? Early experience in the department had suggested that this was unlikely. While there were some exceptions, most departmental architects saw asset management as a constraint on their creativity rather than an opportunity.

Design accountability

One day, as I walked past a design on an architect's easel, I thought I recognised what he was doing. Usually, I had difficulty visualising the finished effect from an architectural layout, so, feeling rather pleased with myself, I turned to my architect companion to check. 'Is that a school with a flat roof and box gutter?'

He looked concerned and promptly whisked me off the floor. He probably thought I was about to query it, and I was. This was a design that regularly caused damage when applied to school buildings, for the school would surround the building with trees, and the leaves would fill the gutters, causing flooding. This costly problem was well-known, so why was it still permitted?

On another occasion, I was looking at a school building design where the architect had, as an aesthetic feature, bricked in the downpipes. I assumed he would have thought about the need to replace rusted-out downpipes at some future time and have made provision for it, but I couldn't see how, so, puzzled, I asked him. Indignantly, he replied that as this was his 'architectural concept', I could not possibly comment!

Architects would often specify non-standard sizes just for variety. This reached ridiculous levels and provoked much hilarity when it was found that the steel plating in the new police building's urinals had been specified at three times the standard thickness! I explained that non-standard sizes considerably increased renewal time and costs, but they did not regard renewal provision as their responsibility. Yet, as is well known today, it is at the design stage that future maintenance and renewal problems are set.

In each case, I asked myself: 'Where is design accountability?'

Service function

Service function was not high on the agenda. I had suggested that we could visit recently designed buildings, along with the architect, to find out from those who were inhabiting the building, as well as those who were maintaining it, what they particularly liked about the building, and what might be causing them problems, so we could learn what to incorporate in future designs. Only one architect was willing.

Would the situation be different in other states? One rainy day, I was in Darling Harbour, Sydney, addressing an accounting congress in a brand-new building. All along the stairs were pots and catchalls to cope with the leaking roof, so at lunch that day with the Chief Public Service Architect, I could not resist teasing him about the inability of architects to design roofs that didn't leak. He professed unconcern.

'Not our problem', he responded airily. 'That's construction's.'

'Not your responsibility to design functional buildings? Then what is your role?'

'We design works of art!'

When asked how many non-functional works of art we could afford, he agreed it was a good question, but it was clear he did not think it a question for him as an architect.

Designs that work in the longer term

However, not all was lost! Although I was consciously looking for it, I was frequently surprised by what first seized people's imagination and created an interest in asset management. For example, when he was introduced to life-cycle costing models and components with different economic lives, our Chief Architect, Peter Sharpe, was intrigued by the possibility of the shorter component lives being used as a defence against design liability. Until then, buildings were expected to 'last forever', and any failure was considered the designer's fault.

With his interest thus aroused, we put together a sample of recent building designs, all award winners, and ran an afternoon seminar for his architects in which we looked at the buildings with an asset management eye. One was particularly interesting as it had won its award for being 'low maintenance'. It was a strictly functional design, but to lighten the effect, a decorative balcony had been added to the top story. This balcony was made of painted wood. When it came time to repaint, it was found that there was no natural access to the balcony from inside the building since it had not been built for use. So, the options were either to erect scaffolding or to remove some of the roofing and enter from over the top. Neither was a low-maintenance solution.

Another in our collection of learning stories was a college for woodworking. The college lay in a heavily wooded area, and the designer had chosen to decorate the façade with alternate panels of local woods interspersed, the better to display them, by white painted panels. The effect was quite splendid — to begin with! But the wooded location, of course, was damp, and it was not long before the painted panels needed a repaint. This repaint could not be done with a spray gun without damaging the strips of local woods; each panel needed to be hand-painted and cut in, a slow and expensive job, especially when carried out on a scaffold. The college could not afford it, and within a few years, what had been a clever design looked sad and decrepit.

After this, we spoke frequently about designing for maintenance and renewal, knowing this would only happen if the client recognised its value. However, as our department was, in fact, the client for many public buildings, we thought we could use our own design briefs to build in a requirement for taking life-cycle analysis into account. One day, the team proudly showed me that they had put out such a brief. But the concept of life-cycle analysis was as new to the private sector architect as it was to our in-house staff. They had no clue what was required of them, and I must admit that the requirement in the brief was not well specified: there was no guide as to how to interpret it.

An opportunity missed and maybe still missing

When the architects who wanted to tender came to me to explain what was needed, I told them that this was their opportunity to demonstrate how their design enabled greater longevity and reduced maintenance. They could think about this when choosing design and fabrics and construction techniques. This, however, seemed to them far too difficult, and they sought a second opinion. Afterwards, I cursed myself for not anticipating this reaction, for it was obvious to whom they would turn, and I knew that had I discussed the issue with him beforehand, we would have given the same advice.

They went to Professor Frank Bromilow, Head of the Architectural Department at the University of Melbourne. It was Frank, along with Lex Blaikie, the Head of the Engineering and Construction Division of the CSIRO in Melbourne, who had invited me to Melbourne over a year before to look at the work they were doing and talk about asset management. When they saw what the PAC had done, they were quick to recognise the opportunities of life-cycle concepts. I knew both would have been delighted at the idea of encouraging better building design and promoting durability and maintainability through the choice of fabrics, techniques, and design, using life-cycle analysis.

However, 'If wishes were horses, all beggars would ride'. In the event, I didn't speak with Frank early enough, and he suggested to his questioning architects that all they needed to do was to spell out the renewal cycle for the components in their design. Which is what they did. After this, I suggested to the team that we avoid building in a requirement for life-cycle analysis in future briefs until I could draft a set of decent guidelines for how this was to be interpreted. Before I could do so, however, I took up a new position in Tasmania.

It was to be almost two decades till I returned to this subject when Charles Nelson asked me to contribute a section on asset management for the first edition of his book, *Quality in Architecture* (2006), and I wrote a section on 'Quality that Lasts'. I later wrote an updated section for his second edition in 2017.

Charles's introduction to my section in 2017 shows that, at least to his mind, closer integration of asset management with architecture was still out in the future somewhere.

He wrote:

> 'Unlike FM [facilities management], the idea of having a role in asset management is foreign to most design professionals. In asking

Dr Penny Burns, founder of AMQ International, to prepare a paper for this book, I hope to extend readers' imaginations past FM, out into the mindsets of those who ultimately create our projects. This represents a further, possibly ultimate 'alignment' of the quality of the design focus with our end users' needs.' (p. 337)

Architects are quite clever enough to do this, but there needs to be an incentive.

Full versions of both papers, which provide a guide and a reason for employing asset management in architectural design, can be found on the Talking Infrastructure website at www.talkinginfrastructure.com/tams.

Audit and accrual accounting

Of course, architects were not the only discipline to find themselves with a new role in asset management. There were the auditors-general and their staff, whom I viewed as kindred spirits. We met frequently to talk about audits and the introduction of accrual accounting. Gradually, they grew to admit its value in revenue-raising agencies — but still, they resisted its introduction in budget-dependent agencies such as education, and I didn't understand why since education had so many capital assets.

I continued to be puzzled by their nervousness till, one day, light dawned! I was addressing a packed audience of public sector accountants, explaining to them why 'tennis tea club' accounting (aka cash accounting) was not appropriate for managing billions of dollars of infrastructure, when a young man asked whether this meant he had to learn a new accounting system. I innocently replied, assuming all public sector accountants had taken an accountancy degree, 'No, you just have to remember what you were taught.'

Ah, the danger of assumptions! It was then pointed out to me that the title 'accountant' did not (in the public sector) necessarily imply an academic qualification, and most public sector accountants did not have it, having learned their cash accounting practices 'on the job'.

At last, I understood. The question was not one of principle but practicality: how were we to educate thousands of public service officers to effect the changeover?

Addressing the practicalities

In conversation with the President of the Accounting Society in Adelaide (I was President of the Economics Society at that time), we decided that we could run a joint seminar focusing on how to make the transition from cash to accrual. He offered to manage the logistics, for which I was grateful, if I would arrange the speakers. Richard Humphry, the former Victorian Auditor General now heading up the Premier's Department in NSW, and Graham Carpenter, the Comptroller-General in Victoria, readily accepted.

The title of our one-day seminar in April 1989, 'Managers and Accounting Information: Making Managers Accountable and Information Relevant', expressed concisely what the issues were, and it had just three sessions: 'What is wanted'; 'What the public wants'; and 'It can be done'. We were able to source two excellent practitioners who had achieved such a changeover within an individual agency, and we could use this as a basis for scaling up. As an indication of the increasing acceptability of the idea of accrual accounting, we had no difficulty securing high-level public sector speakers and attendees.

Also helpful in promoting the idea was New Zealand's Treasury Representative, Ian Ball, who had been presenting seminars on accrual accounting around the treasuries in Australia as early as 1983. The Public Finance Act of New Zealand, which introduced accrual accounting to the New Zealand public sector, was passed in March 1989, thus pre-dating its introduction in Australia. However, in the New Zealand case, this was not related to asset management but to their interest in corporatizing all their revenue-raising departments. Asset management was taken up in New Zealand at the local government level only around 1993 and at the central level much later.

Fund accounting

In the late 1980s, local governments (in Australia and overseas) used fund accounting. In essence, different tasks were allocated a bucket of money and councils reported on this. Also, and equally importantly, revenue inflows were assigned to particular buckets. This had been the subject of criticism by auditors-general and leading accountants for some time. The Australian Accounting Research Foundation's (AARF) Discussion Paper 12 'Financial Reporting by Local Governments', 1988, a significant document in the move to accrual accounting, argued that:

> 'Essentially it [Fund Accounting] reflects the influence of non-accountants. Over the centuries, politicians, lawyers, and bureaucrats have figured prominently in its evolution. For them, legal compliance and accountability were the main considerations. ... What has emerged is more a system of public financial administration, rather than a system of government accounting which discloses in meaningful form the financial performance and position of the executive as a collective entity ...' (p. 23)

The accountants were right to be dismissive of fund accounting. I had already observed how many ad hoc decisions were made by bureaucrats — for example, in determining sinking funds and debt repayment practices in the Engineering and Water Supply Department. While hypothecation, a fund approach, was used for allocating motor vehicle licensing revenue to road expenditure at the state level, fund accounting was much more extensive at the local government level.

Until I moved to Tasmania, my work had been entirely at the state government level, and I had had little connection with local government. I first became aware of the fund accounting practice only some years later. While in America for an American Public Works Association Conference, I spoke with a council maintenance manager. Knowing that American councils were much bigger than those in Australia and wanting to get a rough idea of the difference, I asked him what his maintenance budget was. Puzzled, he started to count on his fingers. As he added up the large number of different buckets, he looked more and more amazed. It was clear that he had previously had no idea of the size of his overall maintenance responsibilities and, equally, no opportunity to optimise them.

Fund accounting belonged to the era of 'stewardship', and in the late 1980s we were starting to move into the new era of 'management'. Stewardship started to be scorned as the practice of the servant who, in the biblical parable of the three talents, buried his gift in the soil rather than using it to improve and grow in richness. Asset management, on the contrary, was directed towards management and active efforts to enhance portfolios.

As asset management grew, so did the need for a better accounting system than fund accounting. Asset management at this time was heavily promoting accrual accounting, which was necessary if assets were to be financially recognised.

Accrual accounting — a change of attitude

Back in 1985, I conducted a straw poll when the National Accountants in Government Conference was held in Adelaide. I asked the sixty or so delegates whom I spoke to what they considered the likelihood of accrual accounting being adopted in government. Their responses very much reflected the general tenor of presentations at that conference, where accrual accounting was considered a theoretical 'maybe' in that they did not see it happening in the near term, if at all. And yet, just a few years later, we were to see a decided change. This is perhaps best illustrated by the following two accounting events, both of which were inextricably linked with the rise of asset management.

New York City, you will remember, had been the first to experience the problems of ageing assets back in 1975 and had struggled with the fallout for ten years. The problems of its largest city led New York State in 1985, under the governorship of Edward V Regan, to move to accrual accounting. The governor wished to get the changeover done in under two years so that it would occur in his first term. It was successful, and he was re-elected.

In November 1987, Governor Regan and his advisor on accrual accounting from the consulting firm of Arthur Andersen & Co were invited to Melbourne by the Australian Society of Accountants to address a special briefing session on accrual accounting. Regan and his advisor spoke of the positive political advantages of accrual accounting, which I thought sensible as many in the audience were members of parliament. However, I doubt the message got through, for when I asked the two politicians seated next to me whether they would consider running on an accrual accounting ticket, the answer was a very definite, 'Not bloody likely!'

The two speakers had placed the focus of their work on accrual accounting at the consolidated state level, which enabled them to show both the assets and liabilities of the state. Previously, the debt borrowings of the state had received maximum media coverage, but the assets that these debts funded had not been recorded. So, the consolidated state balance sheets were very useful for presenting a more balanced account of government activities.

It was also at this time that Graham Carpenter, Comptroller-General in Victoria, showed me the consolidated state balance sheet that he had compiled for Victoria, explaining that the government was often criticised for the extent of its liabilities, but the public and the media did not understand the great extent of assets also held. He wanted to make this evident.

His balance sheet included parks and gardens and heritage buildings — assets that are enormously difficult to value objectively — which explained his first question to me: 'How do we value the statues in the park?' I had not been thinking of the press-relations value of consolidated state balance sheets at that time but of the needs of management and so responded, 'My goodness, why do you want to start there?'

While I could appreciate his aim, I was extremely concerned at the inclusion of assets that could be so easily manipulated to show the state in a good light no matter what its management, or borrowing practices, were like, and I continued to focus on 'renewable' assets — i.e. ones that could be managed.

Accrual accounting and political fears

Hard on the heels of this conference, in February 1988, Nick Greiner, the newly appointed Premier of New South Wales, organised his own accrual accounting session in Parliament House, Sydney. He had made it clear to all that he intended to run NSW as a 'big business' and so was looking to the accounting processes used by businesses. All parliamentarians were expected to attend. The auditors-general and their staff from around the country were also invited. And I.

I was delighted but surprised. When I asked how I had scored an invitation, the organisers said, in a tone of some frustration that suggested they had had considerable difficulty getting all the parliamentarians to attend, 'You're the only one who is really interested in all of this stuff!'

This session differed from that run by the Accounting Society in Melbourne in that the focus here was on accrual accounting specifically for management, using accrual accounting to compare public sector management performance with that of the private sector.

My interest was in the ability of accrual accounting to make the full costs of public activities visible.

But this interest was not necessarily shared by everybody at the session.

In the afternoon, while the audience was being addressed by an academic accountant on the pros and cons of accrual accounting, I noticed growing restlessness amongst a group of politicians at the front of the room. Eventually, one of the politicians spoke up. 'But if we reveal accrued liabilities, we will be forced to do something about them.'

'Not at all,' responded the academic, Bob Walker, smoothly and rather disingenuously. 'Accrual accounting merely presents information. What you do with it is up to you.'

This was too much for the original speaker, who jumped to his feet and shouted, 'You are just like Pontius Pilate, washing your hands of the whole affair,' and he was met by noisy acclaim from his neighbours.

Of course, both the academic and the politician had some right on their side. Accounting systems provide information that enables but does not enforce action. On the other hand, awareness of information can be a propelling force to action; it is the reverse of the old 'ignorance is bliss' argument. If you don't know something needs to be done, you cannot be blamed for not doing it. Once the facts are in the public domain, however, they are difficult to ignore — which, of course, was why asset managers wanted the information.

There was also resistance to its implementation on the part of the Treasury, whose head, Percy Allen, claimed he was far too busy attending to a range of activities, which he listed, to take on accrual accounting. I was disgusted, for none of the items he mentioned, or their totality, came anywhere near the importance for the state to adopt accrual accounting and thus understand the full financial costs of public actions. Fortunately, the premier overruled him.

Accrual accounting — 'It's not asset management!'

The major advantage of using accrual accounting for asset management is that accrual accounting recognises assets. Cash accounting does not. Moreover, in recognising assets, it also recognises the full costs of capital — that is, it recognises the estimated cost of annual asset consumption (depreciation). Again, cash accounting does not do this and, from a budgeting and intergenerational revenue-raising perspective, this is more important than simply knowing asset value.

It was not only politicians who resisted this latter disclosure; many practitioners also did. They were happy enough to recognise the value and extent of the assets for which they were responsible, but not so happy to have to recognise and then cope with the full capital costs. As we noted in Chapter 5, many chose to believe that costs not made visible were not even incurred.

A common view amongst local and state government engineers was that the valuation and depreciation of assets was all 'accounting paperwork' and had no relevance for the 'real' work of maintenance and renewal. A natural extension was to deny that depreciation, which represented the gradual wearing out and obsolescence of assets over time but was not actually paid out while it occurred, was not a cost at all but a piece of accounting chicanery. This view has not entirely disappeared.

Explaining accrual accounting and its relationship to asset management was thus not an easy task. It was a task, however, taken up with alacrity by John Comrie, who was highly influential in the development of both accrual accounting and asset management in local government. An economist and accountant, John was with the EWS when it was developing the asset management prototype. He was then appointed to a committee set up to implement accrual accounting in the local government sector nationally.

He and his colleagues recognised that many assets were long-lived, and to determine costs and charge users on an intergenerationally equitable basis, they would need reliable estimates of replacement costs, useful lives, and annual consumption. Most of John's work was in local government, an asset-intensive sector.

John was keenly involved in the development and implementation of the first accrual accounting standard, Australian Accounting Standard AAS27, and subsequent work. He was responsible for the initiation and development of the local government's financial sustainability improvement-related legislative reforms. These were introduced in South Australia in the early 2000s and were a prime basis for subsequent similar reforms in other Australian states. They included requiring councils to prepare asset management plans and long-term financial plans. It was thus natural that he would join forces with John Howard, Chief Engineer at Devonport City Council, another very early innovator, who was working towards the same objectives at the same time. We will meet John shortly in Part IV.

John Comrie would tell his audiences that 'accrual accounting is not asset management', and, indeed, it is not. Accrual accounting is a financial-management tool. Asset management is a physical-asset management tool. They are related, and there are overlaps. There are also conflicts.

With the decline of fund accounting and the rise of accrual accounting, the accounting profession rose in dominance. As accountants were responsible for deciding the information to include in the balance sheets, their need to report externally, rather than the asset managers' need to manage internally, took precedence, and the conflict between them grew.

This became most evident in the context of understanding asset recognition, valuation, and depreciation, which we will look at in Part IV.

In conclusion, while accounting has grown, and continues to grow, in importance, architects have yet to take the critical active role that could, with other designers, see the next improvement in asset management. Unfortunately, with the increasing privatisation of public audit responsibilities — indeed, the privatisation of public entities — the role of audit, which was so important in the early days, has declined.

CHAPTER 11

REACTIONS

Renewal or maintenance?

I moved to the Department of Construction just before the Construction Ministers' Conference, and my new director submitted my Perth accounting paper as the department's contribution. Concerned that this accounting paper had the wrong focus for construction ministers, I prepared a supplement specifically addressing construction issues. I am glad I did. It was the hit of the conference, and both the minister and the CEO returned well pleased.

This did not mean, however, that the work was understood! 'I'm the envy of all,' said the CEO, 'because at last we have someone who can tell us how much we should be spending on maintenance.' Intrigued, I asked who this was. 'Why, you!' he replied happily. I tried to explain that my expertise was in component renewal, not in maintenance, but my protestations were considered modesty and did not diminish his happiness or belief!

The general assumption at the time was that annual maintenance should be 2%. (Of what, was never well specified.) Now it so happened that the PAC calculations of component renewal had averaged out, across all portfolios, to approximately 2% per year of the replacement capital value, and it was this that was taken as validation of the maintenance figure. It was a misinterpretation, but I could see how it arose. (Later, I wrote an article examining this, entitled 'If the answer is 2%, what's the question?', and this article can be found on the Talking Infrastructure website at www.talkinginfrastructure.com/tams.)

With the large portfolios that we were dealing with, we could predict renewal costs, using the life-cycle renewal model, for we had the economic or useful lives of individual components, and we also knew the replacement value and age distribution of those components.

The reliability of these projections depended on having a large enough portfolio to apply the 'law of large numbers', as discussed in Chapter 6. Renewal projections were estimates of the overall costs to be incurred and not the specific actions to be taken.

Maintenance was different. Maintenance was, and always will be, a judgement call, and it depends on the maintenance policy in place at any given time. Here we have a broad choice between 'run to failure', where failure is not critical nor even expensive; 'maintain at all costs', for truly critical assets; and, for want of a better term, 'cost effectiveness', where we weigh up the costs, risks and performance. Most assets fall into the last category.

No maintenance category is subject to simple cost prediction along the lines of the life-cycle renewal model, so ordinary maintenance was not included in the cost projections. Instead, it was assumed that the maintenance currently being carried out yielded the useful lives that were currently being experienced. Later, this assumption was to be re-examined in the light of appropriate depreciation models and yielded a 15-year research project on 'condition-based depreciation', which we will consider in Part V.

Renewal awareness

After the success of the Construction Ministers' Conference, our minister was keen for me to share the PAC information with his Construction Advisory Panel, consisting of the leading architects, surveyors, and construction personnel in the state. I used the opportunity to stress the need for developing skills in reconstruction. I claimed, brazenly, that 'any graduate fresh out of university can easily design and construct on a greenfield site, but it takes real skill and experience to reconstruct on a brownfield site', and I spoke of the difficulties in reconstructing an existing hospital because of the need to minimise noise, dust, infection, and interference during the daily work of the hospital. I said, this skill was much more complex, and hence rarer, than the skill required to build a new hospital. Moreover, the need for such skill in reconstruction was growing, which I justified with the PAC projections.

This was intended to get a rise out of the audience, and it did. Unexpected, however, was the reaction of the minister himself, who, full of excitement and literally bouncing on the soles of his feet, told me: 'You must tell everyone what you have just told us.' After that, for the next several years in which I was with SACON, whenever I entered a room where the minister was engaged in conversation, he would find a way to change the topic to asset management as soon as he saw me. He was interested.

Regretfully, while asset management knowledge has spread widely, we have yet to reach the public, and until that is achieved, political action will be severely limited. The other problem that we have yet to solve is the ability of the media to easily distort very sensible asset management decisions, as I was to realise in Darwin.

Darwin

I had spoken with the heads of public works in both Sydney and Melbourne before the Construction Ministers' Conference, so they had foreknowledge of the PAC work and had been able to brief their ministers. It was, however, new to the Northern Territory where, some 13 years previously, its capital, Darwin, had been badly damaged by Cyclone Tracey and had required mass evacuations and extensive rebuilding. As a result, a large proportion of its infrastructure was relatively new. While renewal was not imminent, Darwin faced future re-construction peaks when its assets did age.

The Territory's Minister for Construction, previously a builder himself, was particularly impressed with the PAC work and, I was told later, declared: 'We are not going to make the same mistakes as those down south, and we are going to get her to come up and tell us what to do.' And he did. I was invited to visit Darwin for a week to meet with all infrastructure departments and make a formal presentation at the end. I am glad my director was on a long leave of absence; otherwise, I am sure he would have insisted the Northern Territory pay my salary, as a previous invitation to spend just a day with the Victorian Department of Housing had had that response. On that occasion, I had said that, in such exchanges, we gained as much as we gave, so we should not charge.

On my departmental visits, I was surprised to learn that hospitals and prisons came within the same portfolio. 'Why not?' was the response. 'They both deal with captive audiences.'

The main hospital was built to the same design as the hospital in Canberra, our coldest mainland capital, so it was not surprising that the air conditioning was under-sized for the heat of Darwin, our hottest. This was a serious and continual problem, made worse by half of the patients being Aboriginals, who did not like air conditioning at all and would open a window and drag their mattresses to it to get fresh air.

The answer seemed obvious: a choice of natural ventilation or air conditioning. But such was the fear of the political damage that could, and almost certainly would, be wrought by the media interpreting this as discrimination, even if adopted on an entirely voluntary basis, it was not employed.

Interest spreads

Invitations to speak came from all over the country. Each time I would prepare an executive summary for our directors as a way of getting the message across to them. With so much interstate travel, it is not surprising that my fellow branch managers felt a little envious, and the directors also.

One day, word came that the directors were concerned that 'Penny was not doing high-priority work'. That could not be left to rest, so I visited each of the directors, and said, 'I want to be sure that the policy branch is doing top-priority work, so could you please tell me what your top priorities are?' I started with the senior director, the one in charge of architectural services. He looked at me blankly, so to reassure him, I said, 'I wouldn't expect you to tell me off the top of your head [although I did]. What say I come back next week and we can talk about it?' The other directors were no more forthcoming.

So, what was this all about? I think it was my failure to raise the department's profile and, therefore, theirs, though they didn't say this of course. My own director later ruefully declared that he had increased his own profile in the public service but not that of the department, which continued in distress.

The message

I suspect it was general envy that led to my being asked to give an after-dinner address to the Plumbers' Association. Any of the others, all male, would surely have been a more suitable choice to address drunken male plumbers. But I agreed to do it. I agitated for several weeks to find jokes that would be acceptable yet also tell the story I wanted to get across. I tried them out on my daughter, and whenever she laughed but said, 'Oh, Mum, you can't say that!' I would add it to the list.

The main message, of course, was the ageing of our infrastructure, and that failure to attend to renewal would result in the breakdown of many of our assets, including sewers, and lead to regular back-up of sewage in our toilets. This they could appreciate. I told them my jokes, and they were a good audience. However, what I did not expect was the appreciation of the wives, several of whom afterwards came up and thanked me!

They told me they had not thought that a woman would be able to hold the attention of their drunken husbands and had worried on my behalf. (Probably what my colleagues had also envisioned, but I doubt it caused them much worry.) When they saw that I was alright, not only could they relax, but they were proud! In the process, I learned a little about how to talk with practical tradesmen. I also couldn't help thinking that asset management is a natural skill for women who have to manage their own households, and the growth of women in senior asset management positions has not surprised me.

The asset management word spreads

I wasn't the only one willing to take the asset management message out into the world — and doing it. I have already mentioned Roger Byrne and John Comrie. Also amongst the key players at that time was David Ness, the first architect I met in the department and my constant 'go-to' source. He used his position as the editor of *Building and Architecture* to get the word abroad, and later became one of the earliest to complete a PhD in asset management.

Then there was Haydn Reynolds from the water authority. Haydn had a quick wit, and when he saw that forward asset renewal projections rose and fell in a series of irregular humps 'like the Loch Ness Monster', he quickly named his renewal work 'the Nessie Models' and took the idea over to the United States water industry where he was very active. Haydn and I created the 'Asset Managers Forum' in which we gathered all the corporate planning liaison officers from the PAC's work. Later, we invited Adelaide University and the Adelaide City Council to join our monthly meetings.

An engineer who was in the picture very early was Alex Pettlevany from the New South Wales Water Resources Department. Even before the final PAC reports were presented, he approached me with the idea of running an asset management seminar. He wisely involved about half a dozen other departments and organisations to maximise the reach he could achieve, and it is Alex to whom credit must go for the very first asset management seminar, held in Sydney in April 1988. Others claiming such credit at the time were more concerned with maintenance, risk, and reliability — important matters but not asset management.

Of course, we can't forget Professor Frank Bromilow, University of Melbourne, and Lex Blaikie of the CSIRO, who were some of the earliest starters in the game. Later, Frank would arrange for me to meet with his PhD students. They would be asked to explain the nature and intent of their research for me to respond how I saw fit. In this way, we were able to make early inroads into their thinking about incorporating asset management principles in their architectural designs and thinking.

The National Infrastructure Forum

The CSIRO had secured an invitation for me to present to the National Infrastructure Forum in Canberra. I was in Sydney preparing to fly to Canberra when there was an airstrike. I took the bus and sat up all night.

'There, I told you she'd make it!' Dr Selwyn Tucker turned triumphantly to his CSIRO organising team for the forum. It was nice to have a reputation for reliability; however, the downside was that I was asked to change my presentation time from the afternoon to the morning as their guest speaker from the United States had not yet arrived (nor had half the audience).

I agreed before realising I had to follow Barry Jones on the platform. No one would knowingly choose to follow Barry Jones, a polymath, multiple-times quiz champion, member of parliament, and author of the much-vaunted *Sleepers Awake*, on technology and the future of work. He was a powerhouse!

The bigger problem for me, however, was that he was tall. The technicians had extended the microphone to its full length for him, and then reduced it to its lowest level for me. I had only got halfway through my first sentence when the microphone collapsed. Back came the technicians and fiddled around for a bit, and then I had another go. The same thing — halfway through the first sentence it collapsed! Third time lucky, but by this time, my carefully crafted opening was completely shattered.

So when, a few weeks later, I had a phone call from the Local Government Association in Tasmania asking me if I would speak at its AGM and, what's more, 'present that paper you presented in Canberra because few of us would have had a chance to hear it', I saw an opportunity for a do-over and agreed. Then I got on with things and forgot all about it until the night before I was due to fly to Hobart.

With the paper already written, I was about to relax with a cup of tea and watch the evening movie when it suddenly struck me that I could not present that paper to the councils. I had written 'Infrastructure Priority Setting: The Rules of the Game' to tackle what I saw as the practice of the

Australian Federation of Construction Contractors (AFCC) of promoting new capital works to decision-makers regardless of the benefit (or lack of it) to the wider community.

Local councils in Tasmania would need a different paper. So, I heaved myself out of the armchair and retired to my study to rewrite the paper — same title but a totally different paper. Six hours later, I managed to get a few hours of sleep before leaving for the airport. Naturally, when I arrived, all I wanted to do was sleep, so I missed the morning sessions at the conference.

Presentation in Tasmania

There was no opportunity to catch up over lunch either because, at the time, I was in competition with John Klunder, the former Chairman of the PAC and now the Minister for Energy, to see who could be the first to eat in the Members' Dining Room in every state's Parliament House. How this challenge started, I cannot say. Since John had the advantage of his parliamentary position, it was idiotic of me to engage. But there you are! On this day, the Auditor-General had offered to take me to lunch in the Tasmanian Parliamentary Members' Dining Room, so even at the lunch break, I did not hear how the morning sessions had gone.

Which is how I happened to come on stage as the first speaker after lunch and say what I did. Completely unaware that all the morning's presentations had been passionate demands for more money for roads, I opened with a press cutting from *The Courier-Mail* in Brisbane, where I had been a week previously. It was presented as a sad story of how councils in Queensland were seriously thinking about turning their sealed roads back to gravel because they did not have the money to reseal them.

After reading this out, I said that I was interested because roads are a major asset for all councils, and here was an asset management solution to a problem. But, I continued, 'Let's read on.' And, of course, the rest of the article was all about how the federal government needed to give them more money.

'Look,' I said, 'we can throw money at some problems, but we don't have enough to solve all our problems this way. Indeed, I want to tell you there is no more money coming! So you can stop putting your hands out. What is available, those with longer arms are going to get first.' Tasmania, as our top mendicant state, knew this only too well. I continued, 'I want to tell you why this is so, and then what you can do about it.'

At the end of that presentation, John Howard, later to become a leading light for many years in asset management for the Institute of Public Works Engineering (IPWEA), approached me and asked whether I would give that paper the following day to his Local Engineers AGM. It became the only paper I have ever given twice.

That night at the conference dinner, I watched as the ABC reporter moved from table to table, diligently performing his task. When at last he came to ours, he said, with a broad grin, 'Guess what they are talking about at every single table!' For the next several years whenever I visited a Tasmanian council, I would be greeted with, 'Oh, you are the one who gave that paper!'

But an even more interesting result was yet to come.

CHAPTER 12

MOVING ON — MY STORY

The note

It started in July 1989 with a note on my desk that read: 'Michael Weldon, the Minister for Mines and Energy, Construction, and Hydro Electricity, will ring you tomorrow at 9 am about an asset management paper.'

I was annoyed. Obviously, it wasn't the minister ringing but someone from his department and, if only I knew which paper, I could have posted it and saved the fellow the bother of ringing again. Fortunately, before I could say anything, the phone rang.

It was now 9.20 am, and the breathless voice at the other end of the line did not announce himself but simply said, 'I'm sorry to be ringing you so late because now I am late for Cabinet, and I have been late before, so may I get to my bottom line quickly?'

With such an introduction, what could I say but 'Please do!'

'Well,' he continued, 'you probably don't know much about Tasmanian politics — nobody does — but we have just restructured our departments into several large megastructures, and I have inherited the Construction and Mines, Resources and Energy portfolios. Would you consider coming down here and helping me run the show? I don't have time now, but we can talk further tonight.'

That evening we spoke for many hours. He was bright and well-educated. I liked his values and his intentions. And he liked me. We spoke of the difficulties facing Tasmania, the enormous debt overhang with interest threatening to overwhelm the state's income unless it could be cut back.

Tasmania, with a population of just under half a million, had always been a mendicant state, receiving more income from the Commonwealth than it contributed. Now after seven years of construction spending by the previous administration to provide employment (made possible by manipulation enabling the state to exceed its global loan limits), the debt situation was perilous.

South Australia, my state, was also a mendicant state and had been struggling to cope with a reduction in Commonwealth spending. I could envisage South Australia being in Tasmania's position in another few years. Could asset management help in a situation such as this? I spoke with my husband, who agreed this was a wonderful opportunity to explore, and he would do whatever he could to support me. Few could have such an incredible husband! So, when the minister rang a day later and asked whether I could come to Hobart 'and see if I liked the premier' and 'could my husband come too?', we went.

The minister

Although I was there only to consider whether to take the job, the minister acted as if I was already part of his team and asked me to join him in visiting the Water Resources Division. We had just set off when he was called away to a photo shoot. Undeterred, he said, 'You can handle this by yourself, can't you?', leaving me to do the ministerial visitation by myself. Then, as he was being hustled away, he called over his shoulder, 'While you are there, find out about Meander, won't you?' Meander?

Fortunately, I knew some of the water resources personnel from my time at the EWS. 'Relax! It's just me!' I said and explained I was considering taking up a position advising the minister. They were delighted to have a friend in court. While they took their seats, I quietly turned to the minders accompanying me and said, 'How do I play this?'

'Ask them about their money problems,' they replied — a brilliant idea that got the conversation rolling.

Meander turned out to be a proposed dam. Although expensive, it seemed to yield no extra acreage under irrigation nor extended production time, or any increase at all. I reported that it seemed an unlikely starter, and the minister calmly accepted it. I thought this showed economic awareness. However, the dam turned out to be in a neighbouring electorate, not his, and if the money was not used there, it would be available elsewhere. So, what he was really showing was political awareness, and I realised that this would be something I would need to learn too, and fast.

The Premier of Tasmania and his Chief of Staff

That evening, after dinner with the minister, we joined the State Premier and his Chief of Staff for coffee and dessert and more conversation, and I found that I did, indeed, like the premier. I could not say the same for his Chief of Staff, who arrogantly told me, as if he were the one to make the decision, 'You don't want that mickey mouse job over there in Construction, Resources and Energy. You must be the premier's Economic Advisor.' This was a senior position and, in earlier times, something I would have enjoyed, but my interests now lay in infrastructure and thus with the minister's portfolios, so I declined.

Some people do not take rejection well, and the Chief of Staff was one of these. He tried to prevent my appointment on the grounds that I was not 'political enough' to head up the minister's staff (quite true!), but the minister was stubborn, and he knew he needed help. He was also creative. He constructed a new Policy and Research Unit, independent of any department, and appointed me the head of it, reporting directly to him, so it was, in effect, a department of its own. It was a unique position. Had the Tasmanian public service been better organised, I doubt it would have been possible, but there I was, a departmental head (albeit of a very small department) free to tackle any issue that fell within the minister's portfolios. He might not be happy to hear it, but I have much to thank that premier's Chief of Staff.

Whilst this was being sorted out in Tasmania, I took advantage of an offer to visit the warmth of Darwin to address an accounting conference before moving to a Hobart winter, and an incident there is worth recalling.

The capital-recurrent link

A colleague had earlier told me of a speaker in the USA who had earnestly impressed on his audience that 'There are two buckets of money, capital and recurrent, and they have nothing to do with each other!' At the time, I had laughed at this naivety only to find we were probably no better informed, for, on arriving in Darwin, I was met at the airport by a Treasury representative who handed me a flyer announcing that, in two days, I would be giving a talk to the Treasury.

I had not been asked, and this was the first I knew of it. So I was about to decline when I noticed the subject: 'The importance of the capital budget to the Territory'. I spent the next day in the local library doing back-of-the-envelope calculations on the recurrent implications of that year's capital spend. (This was the time of Paul Keating's 'recession we had to have', and interest rates were over 18%.) I took into account interest and renewal, as well as increased maintenance and operating costs.

On arrival, I was told that it was thanks to their very clever economist from my own university that they had managed to increase their capital spend. I said that, regretfully, he may not have done them any favours, and I showed them the implications of this capital increase for their future recurrent spend, up by 2% on the previous year. 'Do you think this increase in recurrent spending limits will be possible?' They didn't.

The reactions were interesting. Senior staff were furious and would happily have thrown me out of their second-storey window. Indeed, the following day when the Director of Finance was deputed to thank me on behalf of the accounting conference, he was still seething and, forgetting that his task was to say nice things about their invited speaker, said, 'Penny Burns was as controversial as usual. I don't believe everything she says. I bet her department is glad she is going!' This last statement left most of the audience puzzled, as they did not know I was about to move to Tasmania.

The junior staff, however, were intrigued and really engaged. They had not previously thought seriously about the recurrent implications of capital spend. Unfortunately, the passage of time has not greatly changed this situation, and failure to take serious account of the recurrent implications of capital spending is still with us.

Anyway, back to Tasmania …

1989 pilots' strike

The day I started in Hobart, so too did the most damaging pilot strike ever in Australian history. It lasted over four months.

The whole of Australia was seriously affected by the strike, but Tasmania most of all, for the other capitals were connected by road and rail. Not so Tasmania, which, at best, had a limited-capacity, twice-daily ferry. Tourism, Tasmania's main revenue source, was devastated. Given their debt situation, this could not have happened at a worse time.

What happened next should have prepared me for what was to be quite a tumultuous two and a half years. I had been in the job only a week when, on the following Sunday, as I was about to cross the road to the cathedral, I was surprised to hear someone call my name.

It was Paul, the minister's Chief of Staff, with the news about the head of the Hydro Electric Company, with whom I had been finalising my office and administrative arrangements. He had been out sailing on the Derwent the day before, suffered a heart attack and drowned.

None of our agreements had yet been put in writing, so I was the only one who knew about them. The administration panicked. They didn't need to. I told them I did not need fancy accommodation — good light was all I needed. I could also easily manage without a secretary/receptionist and a conference room and all the other perks they offered as befitting my head-of-agency status. And, given the budget difficulties, rather than appointing new staff, I said I would second from the minister's portfolios on an 'as needed' basis. All I really needed was a travel budget that would enable me to accompany the minister when required and take advantage of all the help I had been offered by my friends in Victoria and New South Wales. I think they had expected far tougher demands.

Postscript: I think you want this woman

Later, when I had become friendly with the minister's wife, Tina, I discovered what had inspired him to ring me that morning. The Warden of King Island (where Tasmania's delicious Brie and Camembert cheeses come from) had attended the local government presentation I had made in Hobart, the one that had created such interest, and had thought to send a copy of my paper through to his friend, newly elected and responsible for the major infrastructure portfolios. It had a little yellow Post-it Note attached, reading 'I think you want this woman'. Tina said she and Michael both read the paper and spent the rest of the afternoon wondering how they could get me to come down to Tasmania. I am glad they did. That paper is now available on our website.

PART FOUR: INTEGRATION

AUGUST 1989– FEBRUARY 1992

ADVISING THE MINISTER OF CONSTRUCTION, RESOURCES AND ENERGY, TASMANIA

The fourth part of this volume covers my time as Advisor to the Minister of Construction, Resources and Energy in Tasmania, where I explore how asset management can be of assistance to a state in severe financial distress, extending my asset management thinking beyond an individual agency. This is a time of major change in many elements of administration, and I also consider how asset management fits within these wider changes.

CHAPTER 13

THE BIG SHIFT

When I started my work in asset management in 1984, I was driven by questions arising from managing individual agencies' infrastructure assets. I looked at political and economic changes primarily in terms of their impact on agency asset management. However, by 1989 many other agendas were emerging: changes in accounting, audit, regulation, information technology, and treasury management, for example, and I could no longer think of asset management as the only game in town.

Fortunately, in 1989 I took up a position in Tasmania responsible for advising the Minister for Construction, Resources and Energy, which changed my asset management focus from agency performance to what asset management could do for an entire state. Operating at the state level meant giving due thought to those other changes, and it led to my next question:

Q 7: WHAT ARE THE NEW AM CONSIDERATIONS TO BE BORNE IN MIND WHEN EVERYTHING IS CHANGING?

A time of change

With so much happening, I was not the only one to feel overwhelmed. I think of this time as the beginning of 'The Big Shift', which was to continue for another decade and more — a shift from 'stewardship' to 'management'.

Adopting accrual accounting by the public sector was one such shift. Not all accountants were in favour, but the Public Sector Accounting Standards Board chose to go in this direction, seeing an advantage in having the same system of accounting in both the private and public sectors. 'Exposure Draft 50' was released in August 1989. A few years later, it became the Australian Accounting Standard — AAS27, the first accrual accounting standard for the public sector. It applied only to local government, with separate standards for the states and the Commonwealth expected to follow.

'The Big Shift', however, was more than just a change in public sector accounting; it was a series of interlocking elements that had the combined effect of increased commercialisation and the eventual privatisation of much public infrastructure. The change in public sector accounting was just the first of a great many changes that saw 'stewardship' (essentially, maintaining the status quo) give way to 'management', which focused on identifying and responding to change.

Management success was now seen in terms of measurable performance. This performance tended to focus on the entity itself, or its chief executive, rather than the service provided, or community well-being. The latter had been the focus of stewardship. With the introduction of information technology throughout the public sector and the community generally, there was a tendency to concentrate on what could be measured rather than more nebulous 'well-being'. This approach was to dominate policymaking for the next several decades.

The rise of information technology also led to an explosion in data collection. Engineers, with a focus on maintenance and reliability, had been the first to claim the title of 'Asset Manager'. But now, with IT and new data opportunities, many veered off towards a narrower specialisation in the delivery of maintenance and reliability, rather than tackling the broader role of asset management and decision-making. Nonetheless, they kept the new and popular title, Asset Manager. This group became an early sub-set of asset management.

Others chose to specialise in developing software for asset registers to support the new demand for balance sheets or for more specialised application such as pavement management systems. Other specialisations included Information Technologists (IT), Public Sector Valuers, and Financial Accountants.

As is the way of all specialisations, it was often difficult for each to see where their boundaries lay, and each wished to have greater control than others were prepared to concede. For example, it became commonplace for IT specialists to claim they should control asset management because they defined data fields and managed the databases. Asset managers would fight back by pointing out that IT merely managed the data container and did not have the knowledge to make use of the contents.

With these specialised sub-sets, the development of asset management had now to cope with change from within as well as from without.

From stewardship to management

Not all maintenance engineers moved on to asset management, as noted above. But for those who did, the change meant moving from maintenance as a purely technical activity to consideration of the appropriate maintenance policy to meet their agency's aims; in other words, a move from 'maintaining because that's what we do' to 'maintaining with a purpose'. Moreover, with purpose in mind, the focus shifted from the individual asset to the role of that asset in the total portfolio.

At first, asset management was very much a 'side issue'. Engineers retained their primary operational roles and 'added on' a role in asset management. It required them to look at what they did in a different way. This is easy to say and, with hindsight, to recognise. But it was difficult to achieve. The real challenge here was (and still is) understanding the desired business outcomes, for they can be many and conflicting.

For example, in the (predominantly public sector) water industry, desired outcomes include community health, environment, and meeting the demand of a growing population, as well as delivering a reliable service. Into this mix, one needed to add the regulators, who were trying to set and monitor prices using the economic theory of lowest marginal cost

— perfect for a commercially driven private entity, but where did one draw the 'lowest marginal cost' line for, say, a city like Noosa, in Queensland, with both funding resources and public expectations for excellence in environmental stewardship, versus, say, Ipswich, also in Queensland, where the demographics were such that the 'lowest cost wins'?

Accountants moved from stewardship to management with the change from cash reporting to accrual. This also changed the relationship between accountants and engineers.

Accountants had tended to regard maintenance funding requests as excessive, mostly because they did not understand them. This was hardly their fault as the requests were seldom well explained. It was common for accountants to say, dismissively, of these requests: 'They always ask for more than we give them, and yet they always manage!', believing this to be proof of excessive demands. Naturally, this led the maintenance engineers to ask for more, knowing that their requests would be underfunded. In the end, no one really knew just what the 'real' requirements were.

After the introduction of accrual accounting, communication between engineers and accountants increased out of necessity. The most progressive asset management organisations, however, were those where there was a genuine collaboration between engineers and accountants. Key amongst these was the Devonport City Council in Tasmania, which, under the leadership of Chief Engineer, John Howard, and Manager of Financial Services, Bob Boscoe, led the field in producing some of the country's earliest asset management plans and, subsequently, guidance for others to prepare asset management plans.

Audit raises the asset management stakes

With audit, the shift from stewardship to management was reflected in the move from purely compliance auditing with its focus on 'account accuracy' to a new focus on performance, with 'value for money' audits. These audits revealed many cases of what was, in effect, poor asset management, and they encouraged wider discussion of the issues. The change to performance auditing also made audit reports far more readable, entertaining, and challenging. The media had previously ignored the boring compliance reports, but seized eagerly on the more revealing performance audits, examining and commenting on the governance issues they exposed.

This provoked considerable political resistance. In 1989, at the biannual PAC Conference in Brisbane, I passed by a Victorian MP, a member of their economics and budget committee (the Victorian PAC), who had just finished an obviously disturbing phone call, for as he put the phone down, he turned to the only other person in the room, who happened to be me, and exploded, 'Do you realise what our AG is doing?' There followed a litany of the havoc their Auditor-General was provoking with his performance audits.

Since I was very much in favour of what his Auditor-General was doing, I mischievously said, 'I hope you are supporting him to the hilt.' This led to a renewed tirade, and when I observed that parliament had the opportunity to select the Auditor-General, but then it was essential that he be independent, he voiced his solution: 'Next time,' he said with some savagery, 'we will get a hack; that's what we will do — get a hack!'

Their Auditor-General, however, continued to do his job effectively, which led to a period of conflict between the government and the Auditor-General. Since the Victorian State Government was led by an extremely vocal premier in Jeff Kennett, the conflict ensured considerable and continued coverage in the media. Indeed, it even led to a remarkable showdown with a public march on Parliament House in support of the Auditor-General with bumper stickers proclaiming: 'Save the Auditor-General'. For those that did not live through these years, it is all fascinatingly reported in *In the Public Interest: 150 Years of the Victorian Auditor-General's Office* by Peter Yule. Who knew audit could be so exciting?

The extensive media coverage of this conflict brought matters related to the management of public assets to public notice, and this may also have influenced the growth in government reliance on private-sector information technology companies which started around this time. These firms expanded their 'market' to include public sector entities and insisted on using their 'commercial in confidence' contracts to protect their intellectual property. They argued that auditors-general did not have the authority to audit the performance of these contracts.

New demands on accounting

Accountants record what has been spent and can do so with great accuracy. However, with the move from stewardship to management, financial forecasting was required to prepare accrual-based budgets. While this was common in private-sector business, it was an unknown and terrifying prospect for many accountants in the public sector. It led to a demand for management accountants trained to look at future affordability — but recruiting them was a slow business.

(Incidentally, asset management, which developed in New Zealand around 1993, arose from the Auditor-General's recommendation for councils to produce ten-year financial plans. Councils were not required to produce asset management plans, but they soon realised they had no hope of preparing a ten-year financial plan unless they knew what was likely to happen to their assets. It was a very successful, if oblique, way of introducing asset management.)

Of all the disciplines, economists were very late starters and were not really engaged at this early stage. Yet economic ideas, themselves often poorly understood, dominated the political discussion.

What's an asset?

At the time of adopting accrual accounting and figuring out how to produce the necessary balance sheets, the following was overheard in the Perth Treasury: 'Hey, are roads assets?' Momentary pause and then, 'Nah, you can't nick a road.'

Before accrual accounting, the only asset records that most knew anything about were lists of small, portable and attractive items that could be stolen or 'nicked', and so were put on 'stocktake checklists'. In fact, these stocktake checklists were the nearest thing to 'asset registers' that most agencies maintained.

Accounting defines assets as 'future economic benefits controlled by an entity as a result of past transactions or other past events', and there was much discussion at this time about how to identify and measure these benefits. It was, in most cases, easier to measure the cost of providing the benefit. So, on the assumption that any services being provided must be of benefit simply because they were being used, the terms 'cost' and 'benefit' tended to be used interchangeably.

Whether something was an asset revolved around the difficulty of placing a value on it. This was particularly tricky when it came to assets such as parks and gardens, and heritage, for here, while we knew the annual operations and maintenance costs, it was not possible to determine the equivalent of a capital cost. Some argued that a national park could be valued by converting it into land for development, but then it would cease to have value as a park. The problem was the balance sheet. If we had assets, then we needed to show them on the balance sheet, which meant placing a value on them. But for heritage and parks, any value was clearly artificial. Later, there was also to be spirited debate over how we should value the land under roads. Whilst some argued that this land should be valued according to the cost of the adjacent land, others quickly pointed out that this was circular, given that the adjacent land only held value because there was a way of accessing it — that is, by the existence of the road. Despite this, the debate over this issue lasted for several years.

Historical v replacement costs

At this time, valuation problems dominated asset management discussions, the most extensive discussion being around the choice of historical or replacement costs.

Australia is now recognised worldwide as the first to adopt asset management, and two factors gave it a ten- to fifteen-year head start over most others (although New Zealand was close behind). One was the adoption of accrual accounting, but the other, and in the end more significant, was the choice of replacement over historical costs. Neither was adopted without considerable debate, sometimes quite acrimonious.

When it came time to decide whether the balance sheets should reflect historical costs (the price at which the asset was purchased, regardless of how long ago) or current replacement costs (the price that we would now have to pay), there were arguments for both.

Academic accountants favoured historical costs, as these could (theoretically) be verified by the production of receipts. Historical values also remained constant over time, so the values reported one year were consistent with those reported the previous year for the same assets. 'Comparability' and 'verifiability' were both desirable in accounting.

Asset managers wanted replacement values to help them decide whether to maintain or renew. 'But replacement values are subjective!' argued accountants used to preparing cash-based balance sheets. These held that values should be objectively determined. An economist pointed out that while historical costs are objective, the decision to use them on non-current assets is quite subjective. Amusingly, he said that he would mark student papers similarly 'objectively' by throwing them down the stairs. The mark would be determined by the stair on which they fell, with any that fell on the edge allocated to the next lowest stair. The location of the papers could be verified by anyone and so was 'objective'. It was just the decision to choose this process that was subjective.

Historical costs were generally used in the private sector, where assets typically had much shorter lives. In 1992, I was talking with a fellow who was considered by BP Petroleum to be their best-performing Australian manager. The company measured each business unit on the rate of return on assets, valued at historical costs. When a brand new, all 'bells and whistles' plant was established, it was offered to this best-performing manager. And he turned it down. When I asked why, he laughed and said that he may be the best performer on the oldest assets, but he wouldn't be on the newest. He instinctively knew that the practice of valuing assets at historical costs kept his asset values low, which gave him an advantage, but he was canny enough not to say anything, which kept his reputation intact and the faulty performance measure in place.

What data do we need?

Accrual accounting and asset management both needed new and quite large databases. Since it was expensive to collect, store, and manage data, agencies wanted to make one serve all needs. But different goals need different tools, which was not understood and led to much argument and the idea that the other side was being 'obstructionist'.

Public sector accountants needed to be accountable to external bodies such as the Treasury, the Audit Office, or their regulator for what had happened. Their data had to be consistent and verifiable. Asset managers, on the other hand, needed to report internally to the organisation's management to determine what should happen next. They needed to look forward, and for this, they needed reliable and relevant data. Being 'in the right ballpark' is, therefore, fine for the asset manager, for whom relevance is more important than accuracy.

It didn't help that both disciplines used the same term, 'accounting for', but with very different interpretations. I tried to explain the difference to a group of parks and recreation asset managers with a little anecdote.

Understanding different interpretations of 'accounting for'

'When you come at last to the Pearly Gates and St Peter asks you to 'account for' your life, he is not asking for your balance sheet, your cheque book stubs, or your profit and loss account; he wants to know what value you have contributed while you have been on Earth and what you have learnt. When he asks you to account for your time here, he wants you to consider and judge the worth of what you have done. Consideration, judgement, value-add — these are the operative words in the notion of 'accounting for' in an asset management sense, as distinct from simply giving an 'account of' past transactions, as is needed for accrual accounting.

But that is not all. The mere fact that St Peter is asking the question implies something more. In presenting your account, you are also presenting an argument for your admittance to the Heavenly Kingdom. So, to 'account for' your life also implies an assessment of what should happen to it next. It is, in this sense, forward-looking, and carries with it an implicit or explicit action requirement. This is what asset management requires.

The data needs of accrual accounting are very different. Here the task is to show that we did what we said we did, that we acquired assets to the worth we have claimed, and to acknowledge the decline in worth as assets wear or become obsolete — in other words, depreciate. There is no need to justify the asset acquisition or to demonstrate that the level of wear and tear, or depreciation, has been optimised, at least not in the data provided in the balance sheet. The ministers and executives may well be called on to account for these things at parliamentary committees and board meetings, where they will need to call on the information provided by asset management. Judgement and future decisions are asset management issues. Accrual accounting is concerned with what has happened.'

The solution might have been to hold 'two databases', one for accountants with information that was accurate and verifiable, and looked back; and one for asset managers that was currently relevant and future focused. But this solution was expensive and held to be the equivalent to having 'two sets of books', which suggested unethical practice and thus was anathema to all.

Downsizing and information

A major downsizing of the public service, following the introduction of IT around 1989, spearheaded the interest in engineering databases. Considerable downsizing had occurred before agencies realised that, with all their asset information being in the heads of their staff, it was all walking out of the door when they did. Some agencies hired back recently-released personnel to recapture this knowledge. But then they didn't know what questions they wanted to ask. This generated discussion over what information was needed and how it should be recorded.

The upside: A new awareness of infrastructure cost

In 1984, few knew how much infrastructure cost, and didn't even think about it. But as we entered public and quite spirited debates with the accountants on how to identify and measure capital costs and how to record the engineering information that we had previously taken for granted, this awareness grew. And it spread outside the field of asset management.

A few planners started, somewhat reluctantly, to consider the infrastructure costs of their planning proposals. The staff in the Ministry of Planning and Environment in Victoria in late 1989 thought the infrastructure costs associated with the development of the land about to be released might exceed the global borrowing limits imposed by the Commonwealth Treasury.

Initially, they argued the limits should be raised or removed. This only affected the short-term financing question or the state's ability to borrow. When they started to look into the costs involved, not only to establish new housing developments (which was largely the problem of developers) but how much it would cost to support the new developments by way of water, sewerage, electricity, telecommunications, transport, and social infrastructure, and the ability to pay it back (or not) from the increased activity it would generate, they realised that they also needed to look at the longer-term funding question.

When costs had not been available, it was possible to shelve future funding problems. Victoria did not have infrastructure figures of its own, but the figures generated in South Australia for similar infrastructure were considered reliable proxies. Now new issues arose — for example, 'Do we build ahead of demand or wait until the population has increased sufficiently to enable new infrastructure to be affordable?' Choosing the latter option meant that they would not be able to provide everyone with everything immediately. And, if not, then, 'Who would get what and when?'

So, awareness of infrastructure costs introduced these important, if difficult, political, economic, and planning decisions, making asset management a tool for state as well as agency decisions, which we will look at more in the next chapter.

The downside: We all overdid it

As each discipline sought to come to grips with its new responsibilities, it was natural that we all overdid it.

Audit, for example, overdid their requirement for asset registers. I feel rather guilty about this. The term 'infrastructure gap' was gaining popularity at the time, and whilst in the company of the auditors-general, I had exclaimed with considerable annoyance, 'I can't see how anybody can talk about an infrastructure gap when we don't know what we have, and we don't know what we need', the same argument that I had made to the CSIRO.

The auditors-general looked alarmed. 'We don't know what we have? Surely that can't be so!' I assured them it was, as most had only stocktake checklists. The auditors-general acted quickly to recommend asset registers, but it was very much a knee-jerk reaction, not based on understanding what data were required. Little guidance was given. Agencies such as the water bodies were already making headway in determining the appropriate unit of account and asset register detail, but the tendency of the others was to collect anything and everything, just to be on the safe side.

Accountants overdid it by requiring valuation and revaluation with what is now regarded as excessive regularity and, in many cases, at an unnecessary level of expense and detail.

Nor were asset managers exempt. Our major problem was a tendency to collect data without understanding what we were collecting them for and, thus, what level of detail or timeliness was needed.

So, we all overdid it. It was all part of the adjustments we needed to make. It is a truism that the only way to find the boundary is to step over it.

CHAPTER 14

ASSET MANAGEMENT IN A FINANCIAL CRISIS

In August 1989, Tasmania was in extreme distress. Its fourth consecutive year of drought was not good for dairying, one of its major industries, nor for its hydro energy supply. Government borrowings over the past seven years had resulted in dangerously-high debt levels at a time when Commonwealth decisions had sent interest rates rocketing to 18% and above. Finally, a national pilot strike, which would last four months, had just begun and was already drastically harming the island's tourism. Remembering Churchill's admonition to 'never let a crisis go to waste', suggested the next question:

Q 8: HOW CAN ASSET MANAGEMENT HELP IN SITUATIONS OF SEVERE FINANCIAL DISTRESS?

I had been invited to Tasmania with the implicit expectation that asset management would help the state overcome its financial distress. Yet what really could be done? All agencies were in a situation where the needs of the 'urgent' were driving out those of the 'important'.

We often chafe under restrictions, but it can be even more challenging to be unconstrained, as I discovered now that I had the freedom to tackle any problem I could see. As mentioned earlier, my focus, and that of other asset managers, had been on applying asset management to individual agencies, primarily for the sake of improved performance.

In Tasmania, I was looking simultaneously at Rivers and Waters (and thus local government), Mines and Energy (including the state's monolith, the Hydro Electric Commission or HEC), and the whole of Construction, with the responsibility for advising the minister on the impact of each of these on the state. This often put me in opposition to the various agencies as they looked only at how things affected them.

The HEC, the state's major employer and revenue raiser, should have been pivotal to the state's recovery, but it was antagonistic to the government. It held the Labor Party — and especially its partner, the Greens — responsible for its inability to access the very last viable site for a hydro dam in the state. I suspected this was the first time the HEC had faced determined opposition — and lost!

In addition to these broad issues, since my minister drew his support from the unions, I needed to keep them on side. It was a continuous juggling act, not helped by the fact that not one of the agencies — and indeed very few of our own staff — was prepared to recognise the severe financial difficulties that beset the state. The minister and the premier knew, but they had even more balls to keep in the air.

Finding a solution

Solving a problem requires that you first know you have one!

While it was obvious to me, the minister, and the premier in 1989 that Tasmania was in unusually severe financial distress, this, strangely, did not seem obvious to others, and there was no sense of everyone needing to row together to solve the problem. The Treasury acted as if the problem was serious but not critical, even though the current situation could not have continued for another eighteen months without the state becoming bankrupt, such was the rapid rise in its debt and interest payments.

Our own ministerial staff, and others I spoke to, thought the problems were overblown. Being in debt was such a normal condition for the state that no one took it seriously. Later, I was to hear that Tasmania's financial situation was of so much concern to the National Labor Party that it was discussing whether the island had a continued future as an independent state, or whether it might be better for it to become a territory under direct Commonwealth direction or be absorbed within Victoria. Maybe the situation was easier to recognise from the outside? With a population of fewer than half a million, either move could have made economic sense; had this been widely known, it might have generated a greater willingness for the government and its agencies to take on more active and earlier corrective action. But it wasn't, and it didn't.

How had this situation arisen?

In 1978, a proposal to build the Gordon-below-Franklin dam on the Franklin (Tasmania's last 'wild river') to supply a new hydro station was met with a serious environmental protest, led by Bob Brown of the Wilderness Association and supported by the Labor Party, which led to the eventual declaration of the land as a heritage area. In the end, intervention by the Commonwealth Government and the Supreme Court prevented the construction of the dam.

Dam construction had long been one of the major employment opportunities in the state. Dairy, timber, and tourism were the others. Hydro development had started under Albert Ogilvie, Premier of Tasmania (1934–39), who had based the decades-long Labor ascendancy on hydro development to assure full union employment. This policy continued under subsequent premiers and especially under the leadership of Labor Premier, Eric Reese ('Electric Eric', 1958–1969 and 1972–1975). So, seemingly forever, there had been close cooperation between the trade unions, the Labor Party, and the HEC, which was about to come to an end.

The focus on union employment, rather than employment more generally, meant that the government had never seriously considered alternatives to dam construction as an employment generator. The action of conservation groups, supported by left-leaning labor state and federal governments, thwarted the last viable hydro dam in Tasmania and its job creation. The population, experiencing a 10% unemployment level and fearful of losing their children to employment opportunities on the mainland, then switched their allegiance and voted in the right-leaning Liberal Party.

The Liberals looked for alternative infrastructure options to fill the gap left by the absent dam construction. For the next seven years, they funded many capital projects, but few raised state revenues. Instead, state debt levels rose. By the early 1990s, during the 'recession we had to have', interest rates shot up to over 18%, and the die was cast.

By 1989, with the economy already performing poorly and expected to get worse, the then Liberal Government took a chance on defeating the newly elected, and still unknown, leader of the Labor Party by going early to a general election. Had it not been for the strength of the incipient Green movement, led by Bob Brown, still invigorated by its win in the dam case, the Liberal Government's gamble would have paid off. Instead, of the 35 seats, Labor won 13, and with an accord with five independents of Green persuasion, they managed to beat the 17 seats won by the Liberals, so held the balance of power by the narrowest of margins.

Now a very shaky economic and financial situation was left to be sorted out by a very shaky government.

The urgent v the important

Whilst Tasmania's situation was critical, other states also faced budget constraints. State treasuries and financial controllers in infrastructure agencies were seeking ways to reduce costs. Many of the solutions that all states eagerly adopted at this time had some very poor consequences for asset management. A popular choice was to sell off profitable government services, use the revenue for other purposes, and then commit to buying back the original services for an agreed period.

Restrictive global loan limits, combined with decreased grants from the Commonwealth, encouraged public entities to seek these non-borrowing sources of funding, such as selling plant and leasing it back, for a quick cash fillip. Agencies that resorted to such buyback agreements were then locked in for five to seven years and were unable to reduce plant holdings when, with advances in asset management, it became clear that this could be a better option. They were locked in, and it ended up costing them more in the long term. Many were aware of this at the time, but the immediate need was deemed more urgent.

The private sector was lobbying hard to take over any revenue-raising government business. They claimed that public ownership meant subsidisation and unfair competition, and that the private sector was inherently more efficient. The economic downturn thus contributed to the growing privatisation movement.

Asset management was initially seen as a means of cost reduction and eagerly taken up as such by many agencies who did not realise that whilst asset management can, and indeed does, give rise to more effective, lower-cost solutions, it cannot do it from a standing start!

In 1991, British Rail was able to cut its costs greatly by declaring that 'any asset not sponsored by a business must be scrapped'. It required every single asset to be pinned down to a single business and, within that business, to a single owner, realising that common assets 'held centrally' were a recipe for waste. Application of this principle enabled British Rail to reduce its locomotive fleet by 17% and its wagons by 25%.

Such excellent results, however, were only possible because of the extensive research and administration that preceded British Rail's decision. Change of this order takes time and considerable senior-level support. Both factors were missing in Tasmania at this time and, indeed, also missing around Australia as a whole.

Asset management and priority setting

In 1989, asset management was still new and not well understood. Most field officers saw it as a collection of 'doing' activities — namely, maintenance, renewal, capital construction, and operations. Many senior officers saw it the same way. This meant that asset management responsibilities were not allocated to those best equipped to plan and aid decision-making. Instead, they landed on maintenance crews already doing their best under difficult circumstances and without extra resources. Unsurprisingly, a common complaint was, 'I can't even manage with the funds I have now, so how can I find extra for asset management?' and, further, 'In any case, if there are no more funds to do anything, what's the use?' So, many began to see asset management as merely the latest burdensome bureaucratic fad.

Whilst sympathetic, I would say, 'If you can't afford to do everything, don't you want to be sure that you are, at the very least, tackling the most important things and not wasting the money you do have?' It took quite some time until it was recognised that asset management was not a doing task but a decision-making task. It was about deciding what could and should be done.

The South Australian PAC reports on asset renewal had raised interest in asset management, which they did by illustrating the size of the future problems that needed to be managed. The focus was on management, and the summary report was, in effect, the world's first asset management manual, with examples. The aim was to improve decision-making for infrastructure. Interestingly, AM also proved to be of value when it came to human resource management.

When I arrived in Tasmania, the HEC's last two possible dam constructions were finishing. When they finished, many hydro engineers would lose their jobs and leave the island since there would be no other skilled employment for them in their area.

Fortunately, although none of the HEC board members thought that future asset renewal was a problem, there were leading engineering planners in the HEC who realised that once they let their specialist engineers go, they would need to get work off the island and it would take a lot of money and time to get them back again when needed. So, they started wondering what would be the first elements of their plant that would require renewal and when. If they knew this, they could decide which engineers to retain. Could AM help in this exercise? I figured it could, and taught a group of hydro engineers how to do life-cycle costing. By focusing on what elements would need renewal first, they could prioritise the retention of the necessary engineers.

Using asset management for human resource planning in this way was an interesting new application. It did not mean, however, as some enthusiasts started promoting around this time, that it could replace human resource management. The dissatisfaction of many with their human resource management had encouraged the idea of thinking of employees as 'assets' (after all, any number of organisations were saying 'Our people are our greatest asset', so why not treat them as an asset?). But people are not merely physical objects.

A more interesting extension was to take the essence of asset management decision-making — consideration of the consequences — and apply this beyond agency boundaries. My role as advisor to the Minister for Construction, Mines and Energy gave me a unique opportunity to do this, and an occasion arose with Bell Bay.

Bell Bay and the undersea cable

Most of Tasmania's energy is created by hydropower plants, using water stored in dams, and 'run off river', which are available when the rivers are running strongly. There was also an oil-fired plant in the north of the island at Bell Bay. It was expensive to run, so used rarely — maybe only once every four to five years. With the island now in its fourth year of drought, however, the time had come to fire up Bell Bay, which meant an opportunity for the minister to be photographed pulling the switch! He wanted me to go with him to see the Bell Bay plant to get my view on a plan he had. Tasmania didn't have gas on the island, but the minister thought that if a source of gas could be located close enough to be piped to the island, guaranteed demand from Bell Bay might provide a financial incentive. The HEC, however, had planned to develop an oil refinery near the site. The plans conflicted.

This is where the issue stood when, some months later, we received a pre-feasibility study for a proposal to link Victoria and Tasmania by way of an undersea cable designed to transmit electricity both ways. It was a very glossy document. These proposals usually are. After all, their purpose is to excite the imagination and get a commitment. It is also common for them to overstate benefits and understate costs, but this one didn't. It did the reverse, at least on the side of benefits and, as far as we could tell, it grossly understated the benefits to Victoria. Puzzled, I talked it over with the premier's economic advisor and with another senior officer experienced in economics. We agreed that the benefits appeared to be seriously understated. We just didn't know why. With the understatement of Victorian benefits, both sides appeared to benefit equally, but why should that matter? It was not until someone remembered that when the High Court prevented the construction of the Gordon-below-Franklin dam and thus stopped the construction of the related hydro plant, the federal government had promised to pay for the next capacity expansion that Tasmania required. Now it suddenly made sense. Presented in this way, the proposal could be considered Tasmania's 'next capacity expansion' and so would be funded by the Commonwealth.

The engineers in both Tasmania and Victoria were excited by the idea of this project. No undersea cable had been lain at such a depth, over such a length, and in such turbulent waters! It was a great challenge. And all the costs would be picked up by the Commonwealth! No wonder they were excited. Had I been an engineer, I know I would have been too. However, it was a mistake to think that it was at no cost. The funding promise had been to the Tasmanian Government. The funds were, in fact, government resources to be used when capacity expansion was next needed. But was that now?

One of the chief things that good asset management information and analysis can do is to help determine the optimum time for capital expansion. The information available in the pre-feasibility study was sketchy at best. One of the striking omissions had been sensitivity analysis on the load growth forecasts. I now doubted the study's veracity and, given the HEC support for this project, I figured I would need to do such sensitivity analysis myself. I used my friendly backdoor channels to get the raw data and constructed the forecasts. These suggested it would take at least ten years before Tasmania needed to expand its capacity. But now we had a more serious problem.

Everything is connected

I discussed the forecasts with the minister. While not needed now, we could build ahead of demand if we wished. It would not be efficient, but inefficiency would be the least of our worries. I told him that as soon as he agreed to the undersea cable, Tasmania would become part of the national electricity grid. This would mean any future decisions on electricity supply in Tasmania would not be made by Tasmania but by the grid management on the mainland. '

So, if you were successful in finding a source of gas, you would not be able to offer Bell Bay as an incentive, for that choice would not be yours. Worse, not only would you lose control of your energy policy, but at the same time, you would also lose control of your industry policy because you would not be able to bring in gas for industrial expansion. And should Tasmania lose control of its industry policy, it would also lose control of its employment policy and then its economic policy more generally.'

The minister nodded thoughtfully. 'It's like dominoes!' he said. I agreed — and advised him not to sign the proposal. He understood and told me, 'I will not sign until you tell me to sign.'

My confidence in my analysis and load growth forecasts had been boosted by a very lucky break. I was presenting a paper at a conference in Melbourne when I met a fellow from the State Electricity Commission of Victoria (SECV). Naturally, I asked him whether he had any knowledge of the undersea cable pre-feasibility study. 'Why yes,' he replied happily, 'I'm heading it up.'

I quickly gave up a little prayer of thanks and said, 'Please tell me why you have done no sensitivity analysis on the load growth forecast.'

'Well,' he said, 'it is only a pre-feasibility, and we haven't done everything yet.'

'Granted,' I conceded, 'but surely a sensitivity analysis would have been one of the first things you would have done.'

At this, he looked down, took an inordinate interest in the carpet, and shuffled his feet but said nothing for several minutes. At last, he looked up, embarrassed, and said, 'We were told to make it look good!'

I then asked him to join me for dinner, at which my suspicions were confirmed.

I was glad that I had spoken with this nice fellow for, a little later, the minister reported, 'The federal minister is leaning on me.' I grinned and said, 'Lean back.' And he did. The next thing I knew was that John Kerin, the Federal Minister for Energy (and a Victorian), was flying into Hobart to take me out to lunch so he could talk to me, economist to economist!

My first thought was that he intended to overawe me, but that proved not to be the case. He was well-mannered and not at all arrogant. We had a good lunch and talked economics. At the end of lunch, I needed to tell him that I thought this might be a good deal for Victoria; indeed, it could be a good deal for the mainland electricity grid states as well, assuming all went well with the construction of the cable. However, whether the construction went well or not, it simply wasn't a good deal for Tasmania, and it was my duty to act on Tasmania's behalf.

Perspective

All cost–benefit studies implicitly take a perspective. What is a benefit for one may be a cost for another, for benefits are seldom equally shared. Failure to ask (and answer) the question of who is to benefit, how, and why this group rather than another, or the companion question of who will be disbenefitted, often lies at the heart of later social and political problems.

I never did tell the minister to sign and, despite the shouting and anger from the HEC and the opposition, it is noticeable that the opposition, when it took over government a year later, didn't sign either. In fact, it was just on ten years before the cable was finally built. (And a few years after that, the cable failed, and emergency generators needed to be flown in and used for about six months! Compensation from the contractors to the HEC, now 'Hydro Tasmania', and the Tasmanian Government was still outstanding at the time of writing.)

Asset management and organisational structure

Some organisational structures do not lend themselves to good asset management. There are good reasons for suspecting that this might apply to the use by governments of statutory corporations, like the HEC, which lack any detailed accountability. It certainly applied to how the minister's Construction Department in Tasmania had been set up. It was a very odd structure and, ultimately, unworkable.

In 1989 it was the fashion for governments to meld their agencies into mega departments. Everyone was doing it. This reduced the number of departmental heads the minister needed to deal with, and the number of departmental conflicts they needed to be involved in. At the same time, it gave rise to new opportunities for promotion, so it had attractions for both the government and the bureaucracy.

The Tasmanian Treasury was asked to reduce 50 agencies to 20 — and given only a few months to do so. One of the things it was quite proud of at the time was to put all the 'blue-collar' workers from the various departments into one 'construction' department. This department's budget, however, would not cover all these workers — large parts would be left with user agencies, like Roads, and the idea was that they would 'buy' the staff they needed from the Construction Department. The user agencies were also free to go to the market if it thought it could get better value there.

This was seen to provide the benefit of competition. And it did. In theory. In practice, the construction workers, once proclaimed the salt of the earth and reliable hard workers by their previous agency employers, now became, in the eyes of these same employers, lazy, useless, and not 'value for money'. The Roads Department started using portions of its labour budget to go out to the market, which resulted in inexperienced market labour working alongside previous Roads employees. On the roads, this often ended up in shovel fights between the two gangs, which could get quite dangerous and, at the departmental level, the CEO of Construction was left scratching his head about how to pay the wages of his unemployed staff.

After many months of struggle, the department prepared a Cabinet submission to get the situation revoked and funding returned to them, but it was not well-written. The minister gave me the submission, saying that if he took it into Cabinet, he would be laughed out of the room, so asked if I would please rewrite it. He then increased the pressure by saying he was prepared to close the whole department down if it was unworkable, so could I please advise him when he returned from his electorate — in four days' time!

Clearly, the way it was constituted, the department was not viable in the long term, nor was any restructuring likely to be acceptable to Cabinet, but releasing all its workers onto the market would be socially disruptive in the extreme. I recommended a phased approach. To win Cabinet support, I praised its wisdom in separating demand and supply, which was the only benefit I could see in the arrangement.

My opening line was, 'Tasmania is in diabolicals because …' The public servants were horrified at the use of the vernacular in a cabinet submission, and I had not intended it to stay, but the minister was delighted and would not let anyone change a word. 'My colleagues will read this,' he said. And he was right. They did.

Asset management is decision-making

There was much agitation, but little change resulted, and shortly afterwards there was a reshuffle: the minister switched his construction portfolio for police, and I was not involved further.

In New Zealand, the same situation had arisen, and New Zealand corporatised and then privatised its construction department. It became the hugely successful Opus consultancy. Unfortunately, this was not an option for Tasmania because it required a core of strategic decision-makers. When the Construction Department was created, nearly all decision-makers were left with the user agencies, so construction ended up with many doers but few decision-makers. A complete lack of balance!

This was a pity, for the potential for a construction department with sound thinkers is considerable. A good example of this is the work of one such engineer, Peter Cook. The Hospitals Department had approached him to undertake a relocation of the thirty-plus-year-old maternity hospital onto the grounds of the main Hobart Hospital. All they wanted was a simple replication of the existing hospital on the new grounds, which in those days could have happened, but Peter asked, 'Have you done a demographic analysis?' and, from the reaction, realised that they hadn't.

He then pointed out that much had happened in the years since the maternity hospital had been constructed: the population was now much older, and the birth rates were only a fraction of what they had been. Moreover, the road system had been greatly enhanced, and it was easy for users to access any of the new hospitals around the country that had now been established. Technology, too, had come a long way; new hospitals were designed to be both smaller and much more efficient to operate.

Because of his timely intervention, instead of replicating the old maternity hospital, a new one was designed that was smaller, more efficient, and about a quarter of the total capital and recurrent costs that would have been involved in strict replication. That asset management service is what construction departments should be able to offer routinely. We needed more asset managers like Peter.

So, what is the answer to Question 8: What can asset management do for a state in serious financial stress?

Like Peter Cook, it can ask better questions, consider better options, and generate better data. And it can look ahead to the wider consequences of actions taken or not taken. In circumstances where everything cannot be funded (the usual case for all agencies at all times!), it can determine the most important actions to be taken and what consequences will need to be planned for and managed should those actions not be taken.

CHAPTER 15

REACTIONS

As we go through our working day, there are many small things we learn that end up affecting the way we view much bigger things. Here are five of my reactions that I later built into my asset management work.

1. The question of accountability

Not everyone looks at the world through an asset management lens. This may not seem at all strange to most of you. But somehow it did to me.

I had spoken with each HEC board member when I arrived and was disappointed (and rather surprised) to find no recognition of the need to plan well ahead to manage their extensive hydro assets. When I raised the issue of ageing assets, it was dismissed blithely with the statement that everything was under control. There was only token accountability to the minister; in fact, they tried to keep as much information away from him as possible. Only one board member, personally acquainted with the minister, thought this wrong, but if he were to be seen speaking with the minister, he would not have been a board member much longer. I would sometimes meet this fellow for coffee in an out-of-the-way spot, and he would bring me up to date.

When the Labor Government chose to support the Greens rather than the HEC over the Gordon-below-Franklin dispute, cooperation between the government and HEC ceased. So it was that when the government looked to ease its financial constraints with profits from the HEC, it found that the $25 million it was looking for wasn't there. In fact, the HEC had made a loss, which the government, under the rules, was obliged to pay out. One staff member said to me, 'What's the point of making a profit? The government will only rip it off us.' One might ask who they thought the profits of a state-owned enterprise were for, if not for the state.

At this time, governments across the country were enthusiastically setting about expanding the number of their own statutory corporations, believing that this 'arm's length' control would protect them from criticism when difficult pricing decisions had to be made. But without genuine account-ability, where was the incentive to engage in asset management or, indeed, any effort to improve performance?

This was probably as true of private as it was of public corporations, as suggested by a stay at the James Cook Hotel in Wellington, New Zealand. The manager became very excited when I said I was an asset management strategist. He told me that he produced an asset management plan every year, but he could never get any of his board members to show any interest in it. All they were concerned with was the splendour of the foyer and the quality of the dining room menu to impress their guests!

2. *The danger of a single focus*

One day, a Greens advocate, without invitation, sat himself on a corner of my desk for over an hour and proceeded to tell me what needed to happen to protect the Tasmanian environment. This fellow was a double first at Cambridge, so I heard him out. He told me that we must destroy all the maps and remove all the signage, with the aim being to remove all human population from the island so it could recover!

Not all Greens were as extreme as this, but they mostly had a narrow focus on environmental issues and little interest in any social or economic concern. For example, while Tasmania was suffering severe financial stress and high unemployment, one of the newly-elected Greens campaigned to restore Lake Pedder, a lake that had been, many years earlier, flooded for a hydro dam. There was no attempt to justify the cost or the benefits involved, or even to identify them. It was sufficient that the move was considered 'environmental'.

Initially, I was supportive of Bob Brown, the leader of the Greens. This changed after two experiences. The first was at an appointment I had with him. It was at 8.30 am, and I was on time, indeed a trifle early; 8.30 am came and went. Nine o'clock came and went. At 9.30 am, he breezed in, said hello, and breezed out again. 'Isn't he wonderful!' gushed the secretary. 'He doesn't wear a watch!' His lack of consideration was annoying but not critical. Deception, however, was.

Under their 'accord' agreement, the government had agreed to discuss new proposals with the Greens. I was at one of those meetings. So when, the next day, Bob Brown stood up in the House and declared that the government was going back on its promise because they had not answered a certain question, it took all my self-control to avoid shouting, 'You never asked it!' Not surprisingly, the accord was terminated after only 409 days.

I don't know why I expected the Greens to be more honourable, except, of course, that was how they promoted themselves. This is what drove the ministers, staff, and public servants crazy. The Greens always acted as if they were the only honourable people in the room.

3. The source of value and the power of narrative

Truth may be stranger than fiction, but fiction can sometimes have an advantage.

The minister had asked: 'What's the source of value? Some of us [i.e., his cabinet colleagues] have been looking at this.'

I gave him an economics answer, which he understood, but it was clear that it didn't answer his real concern. I was intrigued — a whole group of politicians thinking about the source of value! What could this be about? I thought about it for several days. Then I wrote a short playscript and gave it to the minister to read on his three-hour weekend commute back to his electorate. On his return, he winked at me, took the script out, and gave it to his secretary with instructions to 'Make ten copies. I have some colleagues who need to read this.'

What I had realised was that, with the state's financial situation and budgets needing to be cut, each minister would have been desperate to make the case for the importance of their own area. So, the premise of my script was that it was the end of another long hard week and the ministers were gathered around the bar, arguing who contributed most to the state. Having agreed that whoever could make the best case would be deemed the senior minister, they all set about arguing why they added the most value.

Of course, I introduced a heap of ministerial portfolios that didn't exist to avoid offence, and my minister had all the best lines. But the twist was when they realised that while they might not have the resources to add value by doing more, they could still add value by doing less! Or by prioritising and removing what was of less value than it cost to provide. Fragrance-free soap, after all, is sold for a higher price than perfumed soap. Could we also increase value by removing activities that were not highly regarded? The script ended with them vying for who could do the most for the state by removing what had no or little value.

This was easier in the fictional world than it was in the real world. But it was fun, and it set the idea in motion. This script is available on our website.

4. The importance of the non-obvious

As mentioned above, towards the end of my time in Tasmania, there was a reshuffle, and my minister swapped the construction portfolio for Police and Emergency Services. I told him I feared I would be of less value to him in this new role. 'Nonsense,' was his immediate reply. 'You will see what the others do not.' And he promptly placed me on a Commission of Inquiry into the Police.

At our first meeting, the Police Commissioner, who, much like all police commissioners, did not care for civilian overview, and even less for female civilians, glared at me for quite a while. Eventually, he said, 'I do not know why you are here!'

Fair enough. However, I could hardly tell him I was there because I would see what the others did not. So, after a pause, I said quietly, 'No, I guess you don't.' That non-committal response not only had a powerful impact on the Police Commissioner but on the other Commission members as well, who were probably thinking the same thing. Since I only reported to the minister, there was no need to account for myself to others. But it was an interesting example of saying more by saying less.

It was also recognition that it pays to be on the lookout for the non-obvious. For example, was it possible to reduce the state's cost by reducing some of our extensive police housing? Could we perhaps rent when needed? 'No, we can't,' they said, 'because if we have our own house, then everybody knows, and it becomes a second, de facto, police station.' But do we really need two police stations in our small country regions? As I pressed on each response, I would be given yet another reason, no more valid than the one before.

Curiously, when the truth was eventually and reluctantly revealed, it was something that I could recognise as being valuable. Some police, while valuable, were hard to discipline, and the trump card the Police Superintendent had to hand was, at a moment's notice, to assign the troublesome officer to one of their more remote locations. That, however, only required a few readily available locations. Not all regions needed their own housing. And so we came to an agreement.

5. Where a focus on construction leads to waste

The question that the minister had asked me on my very first day was about Meander, which turned out to be a dam that would enable no new irrigators or extension of growing time or, indeed generate any extra income. So why was one of our officers, a Rhodes Scholar and no idiot, campaigning for it so strongly? We spent many hours arguing over this before he eventually said, 'Look, we are going to spend the money somewhere, so it might as well be here!' Where did this idea of inevitable spending come from?

On another occasion, I was asked to join a small group to help the roads department decide which of five roads they should choose to build. I could not see a case for any of them, so I asked the facilitator why these particular roads had been chosen. He sidestepped the question. I asked again. Same reaction. So, I boxed him into a corner at the tea break and told him there was no way I could take part in this exercise unless I knew the rationale for the road selection. The answer, when it came, was as strange as the facilitator's acceptance of it.

Apparently, whenever a roads minister came up with an idea that the department's officers thought crazy, rather than give the minister a clear reason for rejection, they would say that there were insufficient funds, but that they would 'put it on the list'. These projects were all 'on the list', but no sounder now than when they had been placed there. There was desperation in the department to build something — anything. And this was not only for roads.

For this volume, I contacted Michael Field, who was premier at the time I was in Tasmania. He told me that shortly after he took up office, he was approached by the HEC with a proposal for a new plant. He was told that all production could be sold to Alcoa for just the interest cost. Why was that considered a good deal for Tasmania? That question was neither asked nor answered. It was enough to be building something. What was the community value of whatever was being constructed? This seemed never to be considered.

I realised that, whilst construction served a one-year labour demand fix, with benefits to workers, it was generally the big end of town that reaped the real benefits year after year.

There was much that I learnt during my time in Tasmania that was to influence the way I thought and worked from then on.

CHAPTER 16

MOVING ON — MY STORY

In 1991, the Premier of Tasmania, Michael Field, took his cabinet and some Greens on a road trip, speaking to the community across the state, explaining the seriousness of the financial situation. The actions he took then did help to bring the economy back into some semblance of order, and he is now recognised and appreciated for this by those who understand these things. The correction was painful for the people, however, and the government lost support at the election held early the following year.

As I had requested that my position in Tasmania be as a public servant rather than a political appointment, I only had a watching brief for this election. I was struck by the ability of the Labor Party members to suspend disbelief. Later, I realised that this must apply to all elections. Although their chance of success was almost non-existent, they had to believe they had a chance in order to put their all into it. The subsequent collapse was inevitable, and I felt very sorry for them. They had done the best they could for the state, but it wasn't enough, and they were not appreciated for what they had done.

On the night that the results were known, and the members and political staff were commiserating over drinks, I did not join them but rang Tina, the minister's wife, to see how she was taking the news. We talked for over an hour, for it is not only the elected members who put their life on hold.

I still had six months to run in my three-year contract, but the minister agreed it would be a good time for me to go to the mainland and see what else was on offer, and since I had a conference to address in Canberra, I chose to take some time off in Melbourne and Sydney en route. I didn't really know what kind of work I wanted, but my time in Tasmania had given me the freedom to pursue issues I thought were important, and I wanted that to continue. I got this in spades!

In Melbourne, on my first day, I was approached by the Royal Melbourne Institute of Technology (RMIT) to head up its bid for a Centre of Excellence in Asset Management. The Commonwealth Government was keen on promoting these centres, which required the involvement of academics from several universities, as well as participation by private businesses. The grant money was good and competition was high. To encourage me, I was offered the position of Professor of Civil Engineering! I declined the professorial position, but I did say I would be happy to work on a part-time basis to help the RMIT set up its centre.

The idea was well received by the private companies I approached, but the academics had difficulty deciding what to do. I suggested to them that, as they had all been teaching for some years, perhaps they could consider offering advice on the building techniques that had been discarded and replaced by new techniques. Since they would know the reasons for discontinuance and the problems incurred, they could use this to predict future problems of structures built with these techniques. I still think this could have been useful, but they explained that the years of experience that enabled them to know also meant there was not enough working life left to do the research and then benefit from it. It made sense, but since they had no better ideas, that is where, a few months later, the proposal stopped.

In Sydney, on my second day, came an offer to join the NSW Public Works Department, but I had enjoyed my freedom in Hobart too much to now rejoin the public service. The department wanted my help to create the state's asset management manual, so again, I offered to do the work part-time. I had been living apart from my husband for over two years whilst working in Tasmania, and it didn't seem fair to him to now set up a permanent camp in either Melbourne or Sydney.

In Canberra, on my third day, I was offered a role in a consultancy firm, which I did not accept. But it gave me an idea. While I had not previously thought about consultancy, it now seemed the logical route forward, but on my own.

So I returned to Hobart, happy in the knowledge that I had an interesting future. I didn't think the new minister, Robin Gray, would want to keep me as an advisor. He had previously been the premier in the government responsible for running up so much debt, and I had been known, on occasion, to ask him pointed questions at public meetings. I expected to be paid in lieu and allowed to leave the island.

However, this appeared not to be the plan. Word came to me that the intention was to keep me on staff, pay me my salary, but give me no work to do. I felt pretty sure Robin Gray would not have been so petty and figured it must have been his new staff. In any case, this could not be left unaddressed. I walked around to Robin Gray's office, knocked on his door, and smiled at him brightly. 'Hi, I guess I am on your staff now!' It was not too long before arrangements were made for my departure.

As the changeover to the incoming government had now taken place, there was nothing for me to do but pack and leave. But before I left, I wanted to do something I had not had the courage to do before. The head of Resources and Energy had taken an absolute dislike to me the very first day we met, and things had not improved. I did not want to leave without taking one last chance to resolve whatever was the cause. So I rang him and told him I was leaving at the end of the week and asked might I take him to lunch before I went. In the change of government, he had lost a few of his roles and was obviously still seething, for his reply was a not-so-gracious, 'Well, I guess I could. There is not much to do around here.' Rather than risk continuing the conversation, I quickly thanked him and said I would make the arrangements with his secretary.

When we met for lunch, his first question to me was, 'How do you know the minister?' I explained that I had presented a paper that seemed to suggest I might be useful in coping with managing infrastructure in difficult financial times. The warden of King Island, who had attended my presentation, was a friend of the minister and, when he knew he had scored the construction, mines and energy portfolios, had sent him a copy of my paper with a recommendation to get hold of me. He did.

'So, you didn't know him before?'

'No, never seen him or spoken to him before then.'

I don't think I have ever experienced such a rapid transition in attitude on the part of anyone. He relaxed and smiled at me for the first time. Lunch went on for two and a half hours. At last, reluctantly, he said, 'Well, I guess I must get back.' We had enjoyed ourselves, and I wished I had done this months ago. I was still none the wiser on why he had been so instantly opposed, but I was shortly about to find out.

It was now 3.30 pm. I had nothing to do until my flight at 7 pm, and I was feeling sad about leaving the island I had enjoyed so much. What I needed was someone friendly to talk to and have a drink with, so I rang Paul, who had been the minister's first minder and someone who had helped me find my feet.

As we talked, I told him about the curious reversal at lunch and the quick reaction of Robin Gray when I announced my readiness to work for him. Paul grinned at the first story, and his grin widened with the second. Then he explained the luncheon. 'He thought you were Michael's mistress!' I was shocked. It had never occurred to me. Stupidly, I had thought that my PhD would have explained why I had my position. I had been so careful in protecting Michael from the spiteful comments of the media that on the few occasions when I had invited him to dinner at my place to go through thorny issues without distractions, I always had his chauffeur join us. But I hadn't thought that I needed to protect myself.

Why should people have been so quick to assume? Paul had the answer to that, too. 'As to Robin Gray, he would have wanted that office and role for his mistress.' Apparently, this was widely known, so perhaps it was assumed that all ministers worked the same way. Mine didn't. On the plane home, I reflected on some unexplained comments and reactions, and now they all began to make sense. Clearly, the head of Resources and Energy had not been the only one with this view of me. The HEC did, too, as did many of the wives of senior officers.

The creation of my research unit, which placed me in the situation of head of department, albeit a small one, was unusual. I knew how it had come about, but others didn't. Then again, my position as a public servant responsible only to the minister was unusual, as was my ability to determine for myself which issues I addressed. So, with hindsight, I could start to see why this interpretation arose. I demanded of Paul why he had not told me earlier. But he only smiled. As I thought it over, I was glad he had not told me. What could I have done? It would have made my relationships all around so much more difficult.

Bob was at the airport to meet me. Our time apart had made me value him more, and we were closer now than ever. It could so easily have gone the other way! That evening I was more than happy to return home.

PART FIVE: INTEGRATION

APRIL 1992– APRIL 1994

INDEPENDENT ASSET MANAGEMENT STRATEGIST AND INFRASTRUCTURE ANALYST

In this final part of the volume, I look at some of the issues that arose once I was an independent advisor with my own consultancy. By this time, awareness of asset management was spreading widely across Australia and New Zealand, and I considered it my role to promote this spread.

CHAPTER 17

SPREADING THE MESSAGE

My return to Adelaide in early 1992 coincided with increasing public sector interest in asset management. I was giving at least two to three presentations a month. I would also fit in half a dozen visits to agencies such as Treasury, Public Works, Power and Water, Roads, Housing, or Health whenever I travelled interstate, which was much of the time. I was busy.

They would tell me what their problems were and, if I knew, I would tell them how those problems were being tackled elsewhere and who to talk to.

Later, this led to the idea of producing a newsletter to spread the ideas more widely, and in March 1994, I published the first issue of *The Asset Management Quarterly*. By 1999, there was so much information to share that our quarterly publication became the fortnightly *Strategic Asset Management*, available both in print and online, and we created a website, the first to be dedicated to infrastructure asset management and free to all. With the launch of ISO 55000 in 2014, I would choose to switch direction and focus more on the broader question of decision-making for infrastructure. But that was still in the future. In 1992, I found myself most concerned with my next question.

Q 9: HOW CAN THE BENEFITS OF ASSET MANAGEMENT BE BEST CONVEYED TO THOSE WHO DO NOT YET KNOW?

The most obvious first step was to get their attention.

First, get their attention

New assets were always considered exciting, but maintenance and, by extension, management were considered basic and boring. So, to get attention I would do the unexpected. For example, at a conference of public administrators I presented as a game show host, telling them that a similar audience was given the chance to choose from among three boxes labelled 'money', 'labour', and 'asset management'. Most had chosen the first, labelled 'money', but it was empty. Others had chosen 'labour' but that, too, was empty. Only one had chosen 'asset management' and he had said that at first, he was going to pass on that one because he knew that assets were sunk costs and you could do nothing about them. But then, he stopped and realised that he had always thought that, and maybe it was now time to think differently. And this box was not empty.

The difficulty in those early days was overcoming pre-existing ideas. But once done, there was often great enthusiasm. My normal approach was to tell stories.

There was one about the engineer in the boiler room of a cruise liner. When he got the order from the bridge to go 'full speed astern', he queried it, knowing the enormous damage that could ensue. The order was repeated, but the engineer, being cautious, reversed slowly — and the liner ran into an out-of-control yacht, killing 19 young people. The moral of the story was that the one who should make the decisions is the one who can see the issue most clearly.

However, to show I was not anti-engineer, I would also tell another cruise-liner story. The liner had hit a rough patch of water, so the stabilisers had been activated. But the accountant argued against this, pointing out that it would slow the passage and they would arrive late at port, which would be expensive. So, the stabilisers were removed, with the result that the ship arrived on time in port. However, the passengers were so miserably seasick that they vowed never to go cruising again.

This story had two corollaries. One was that, as the rough patch only lasted a short while, they could have made up the time, illustrating the dangers of straight-line extrapolation. The second came courtesy of my husband, who declared that with everyone seasick, the bar takings would be way down; however, an extended time at sea would have increased them, which gave me a splendid example of the impact of thinking only in silos.

Yes, the stories were silly, but each had a message, and the silliness itself helped them to be remembered.

In those early years, honesty generally prevailed. Speakers would not pretend that everything they tried worked, for they were seeking answers to their challenges. However, later, when public relations got involved, the formal presentations would often be sanitised, with the real story only emerging over coffee or dinner.

We all knew about things going wrong, but there was a dearth of happy success stories — successes that could be proved with data. The benefits of asset management were considered to arise in the long term, so we thought we had not had enough time to produce success stories with costs and benefits. It was not until I was put on the spot to do just this that I realised I could.

When you believe you can, you can

It happened this way.

In the 1992 Victorian elections, the voters chose a Liberal-National coalition after 12 years of Labor rule. Politicians have a term for the time they spend in opposition. They call it 'being in the wilderness', which certainly describes the lack of government information available to them.

To overcome this lack, the incoming government instigated an 'audit' or examination of the state's finances.

The NSW Government had done the same thing when their elections, some four years earlier in 1988, had resulted in the Liberals 'coming in from the wilderness', and over the next ten years, every state adopted this practice.

The Victorian Audit was the first to have an entire chapter on asset management, and every state audit after this did so too. I was responsible for drafting the Victorian chapter.

When I was first approached by the steering panel, the key question was, 'How much money do you really need to make improvements with asset management?' — a question that showed they didn't really understand what asset management was. Looking at the long list of tasks the steering panel was considering, this became even clearer, and I was on the point of confessing inability when I was asked to meet the chair of the Audit Commission, who was then Sir Roderick Carnegie.

His assistant had warned me that Sir Roderick could be abrupt, even to the point of rudeness, and I was told I should not take offence. I am glad I had the warning.

He led off with a brusque, 'What's this AM stuff all about?', but I had barely uttered a sentence in reply before he interrupted, irritably, with 'Forget that; just tell me who is doing it all right, and I will go and talk to him.' Him?

Patiently, I tried to explain that no one was doing it 'all right'. 'The water boards in each state know each other very well, and if anybody had got it all right, the others would be beating a path to their door. But they aren't! This is also true of the roads boards. They are in constant communication, but no one has solved all the problems. Some are doing some things very well but struggling on others.'

I then spoke of a few areas being improved by asset management. He accepted defeat, but he was a hard-headed businessman not interested in nice statements; he wanted facts. I was told that my report must include at least half a dozen 'fully costed' examples of good asset management.

And, as he was about to leave the room, he added, 'And I don't want them all from New South Wales.' At that time, I was drafting the NSW Total Asset Management Manual, and Victorian–New South Wales competition was strong. Feelings ran high on both sides of the border.

Asset management success stories

Sir Roderick's challenge to find costed asset management success stories seemed close to impossible at the time, and I have been on the lookout for them ever since, even creating 'The International Asset Management Competitions' in 1996 to help in the search. Here are some from the Victorian Audit Commission. The savings may seem small in today's dollars, but in 1985 and 1990 dollars, they were substantial.

Roads — Projecting the renewal costs of country roads over the next twenty years, based on current life estimates and maintenance and renewal practices, made it obvious to the Roads Department that they had a serious problem. By adopting more appropriate (lower) standards for country roads, which had less traffic, the department reduced the amount of replacement required and postponed the time of peak demand.

Current practice was to replace all country and city roads at around 35 years. Now, when road usage was considered, it was clear that rural roads might last even past the age of 60 years. The benefits of this change were equivalent to an annual saving of 0.5% of the total stock, which equated to more than $20 million (1985 dollars) annually.

But it did not stop there. The Department of Road Transport then carried out research into new road replacement technologies and management techniques.

Incidentally, when I was conducting the research for the Roads Replacement Study for the PAC, I asked the leading engineers what they thought the right amount of maintenance was. They promptly told me that it was the amount they were actually spending.

But I knew these fellows, for we would regularly drink together after our monthly corporate planning luncheons and discuss the problems of the day, so after a few moments, the head of the group relaxed, grinned, and said, 'You know, if you had asked that same question ten years ago, we would have given you the same answer. Yet we are now spending less, our portfolios are larger, and the assets are older!' At that stage, they knew what factors were important but were still ignorant of the consequences. After the renewal-cost modelling work we'd done, they were no longer ignorant.

Waste management — By 1990, Brisbane was growing rapidly, but the city council didn't have enough waste management capacity to accommodate the growth without acquiring more land and building new treatment works. This would be both expensive and time-consuming, so it took a new and innovative approach.

It employed young, scientifically trained officers to advise firms about waste-minimisation measures and cooperated with industry on waste recycling and pre-treatment to reduce the load on municipal treatment plants. Sewer losses of specific valuable raw materials and products were quantified, helping the industry improve its loss-management procedures. This approach, together with pricing and regulation, minimised waste-treatment services and limited unnecessary expenditure on treatment equipment.

Cooperative waste minimisation resulted in a reduction in trade waste equivalent to a domestic sewerage load of 100,000 persons. To have achieved the same result with a capital works program alone would have required an additional capital expenditure of at least $15–30 million (1985 dollars). In addition, generation rates of the more difficult hazardous wastes were reduced by almost 75% over five years. This represented a considerable saving on annual recurrent costs.

Key to asset management success—willingness to seek alternatives

Changing management practice was often better than asset creation. For example, a regional motor vehicle registration office thought it needed more space to accommodate all its clients during peak periods. However, by sending bills more frequently the size of the peaks was reduced to a level where they could be accommodated with the existing space.

The Port of Melbourne Authority had insufficient lorry-holding space so it asked itself what if it changed its lorry pick-up system from lorries waiting for their client-designated load to the system used by taxis, whereby the next lorry picks up the next load, which could result in speedier deliveries, lower customer costs, and obviate the need to extend holding space.

After several capital-intensive options had been considered for reducing salinity in the River Murray, the most cost-effective solution was discovered to be a simple change in management practices by flushing the lake at the river mouth in times of high flow.

Resource-sharing was another popular option and widely adopted — for example, by using milk bars and supermarkets to sell bus tickets and the post office for general bill-paying, customer convenience increased, and many local agency offices could be rationalised.

Once we stopped focusing on construction alone, we realised that a combination of solutions might often be the best answer. For example, when the electricity trust re-examined its demand projections, used demand management, and increased the utilisation of its existing assets, it was able to defer the construction of a new power station, initially for 12 years and then not build at all. It saved annual interest costs of $12 million (1985 dollars) and then the capital cost of a new power station, which was about $500 million (1985 dollars).

These stories were good for asset management, and I and many others started to use them in our presentations.

A few years later, South Australia's government changed, and it was its turn to commission an audit. Now it was clear that attitudes were changing. No longer satisfied with simply collecting information, this audit commission was anxious to engage in asset management research and analysis, indicating how AM had risen in relevance as well as usefulness.

I was fortunate to be given one of the most interesting research projects it has been my pleasure to pursue. I was asked to select four recently completed large projects — if possible, those that had also carried out a post-completion review — and to examine the key decision points in each project and how those decisions had been made. Earlier, it is most unlikely that this question would have been asked. This project was extremely valuable for me and greatly helped my knowledge of, and interest in, decision making.

The audit commission's reports were hardly bestsellers, and they made little impact on asset managers at the coal face. They were, however, keenly read by the lead decision-makers in each agency in their own and other states, enabling asset management ideas to reach senior levels of government and politicians. What they particularly influenced were governments' attitudes to capital.

Attitudes to capital

At this time, most agencies still viewed infrastructure additions as if they were lottery winnings: you put in your bid, and if your number came up, you won. If it didn't, you wouldn't analyse why — you would simply try your luck again next year. Until the Victorian Treasury developed its Investment Logic Mapping approach some years later, few thought about how they could improve the chances of any individual bid being successful. Instead, treasuries, in preparing their capital budgets, received a barrage of hopeful bids. Hundreds of them.

As an economics student, I had thought that engineers would carefully assess each bid proposition for physical success (both efficiency and effectiveness) and that the only task for economists was to determine whether it could be afforded and, if so, what priority it should be given. But years of working in departments had caused me to doubt this assumption.

Working on the audit commission research project mentioned above, I discovered that, with the interesting exception of ETSA (Electricity Trust of South Australia), there was an almost complete absence of an analytical review of capital bids at the corporate level. No one was double-checking the assumptions made, or the data supporting them, for accuracy or relevance.

ETSA, however, had taken the trouble to teach the bidding groups in its large organization how to prepare and check a cost–benefit proposition before it was submitted in-house. This process then left the corporate planning group free to act as a devil's advocate. As a statutory authority, ETSA did not depend on the Treasury for its capital budget. It created and managed its own revenue and expenditures, and carried out its own analysis and review.

When I discovered that there was only one Treasury officer in South Australia whose job it was to check all the capital bids coming before the government, I was curious to find out how he did it.

'That must be a massively time-demanding job for you,' I said.

'Not really,' was the reply. 'I just need to check that they have put something in all the boxes.'

'You mean you don't need to check accuracy and relevance?'

He was not overly concerned. 'No, it wouldn't be possible anyway.'

And so the lottery-winning viewpoint was sustained. It really was the luck of the draw.

To change this, we needed to develop a compelling narrative.

A compelling narrative

Many maintenance engineers, who had been trying to convince their organisations for years that their assets were degrading and more needed to be spent on maintenance, would later ask me why their organisations listened to me and not to them. A reasonable question, for they knew far more about their assets than I did.

At first, I would simply say, 'I spoke their language — dollars.' The maintenance engineers would speak in detail about what needed to be done but in engineering terms, which the managers did not understand. This, however, was only part of the answer; there was more. The major contribution of the PAC was that it had produced a compelling narrative — with data to back it up.

The story we told was that our current renewal represented the ageing portion of a very much smaller stock of assets we had some fifty or more years ago. But over the last fifty years, spurred on by the needs of refugees, immigrants, and the baby boom, our population had exploded, and so had our infrastructure — in fact, infrastructure had grown much faster, and even when the population growth rate slowed and the need declined, it continued to grow. This additional infrastructure, however, was now itself ageing.

If our current practices were unchanged, the rate of required renewal was set to triple and then quadruple within the next twenty years. In fact, renewal would end up being as large as our current total capital expenditure, assuming this remained constant. This was an important assumption because the Commonwealth was already cutting back capital allocations to the states. The increased need for maintenance, which all infrastructure agencies were now experiencing, was, in fact, just the beginning of the wave of increased renewal to come.

Future renewal might leave little scope to acquire new assets but, we emphasised, this was not the time for panic. We had about fifteen years to get our house in order before asset ageing would impose major strains upon us.

So, it was not a time of crisis, as it had been when a similar situation affected New York. Rather, it was a time for asset management planning. It was worth recognising that over 98% of the infrastructure we would need next year was already in existence, even in the highest capital growth periods, so we had scope to switch some of our attention from the less than 2% of new capital to preserve the more than 98% of existing assets.

This was a very compelling narrative. However, asset managers did not have the whole game to themselves and there was a counter-narrative.

Every story needs its heroes and its villains

Our heroes were the asset managers who sought to provide good service, and the villains were those who acted in opposition to sound asset management, either accidentally or deliberately.

During the growth years, when governments had been vastly increasing their infrastructure holdings, they had called on the help of large construction firms that had grown in size and influence. They now formed the rich, powerful, and influential Australian Federation of Construction Contractors (AFCC), whose emphasis on construction alone had led me to write the paper that I presented to the Infrastructure Forum and that eventually took me to Tasmania. Asset management led to assets lasting longer and non-capital options being sought, so it was antithetical to the contractors' business growth model.

Starting in the late 1980s, the AFCC marketed its major campaign which argued that expenditure on new capital had declined as a proportion of gross domestic product (GDP) — measured at its peak in the 1960s! — and that was the reason why economic growth itself had slowed. The AFCC wanted governments to build more.

A moment's reflection, plus a modicum of understanding of asset management, shows that this argument was more than just self-serving. It was ridiculous.

When we build a new asset, the item increases GDP — but only in the year of acquisition. However, the need to operate, clean, secure, and maintain that asset will generate production every year that it remains in operation.

Some assets, such as roads, did not have extremely large flow on, or recurrent operation and maintenance (O&M) costs, as a percentage of capital, but most other asset investments did. For hospitals and schools, the annual recurrent expense could easily be as much as 70% of the initial capital cost because of the cost of staff and consumables. (So much was this the case that when I was working on the PAC study, the health managers thought I was wasting my time looking at capital costs because, for them, this was nowhere near their main expense, despite the cost of new hospitals.)

This meant that just one capital investment in health or education of, say, $100m, in year 1 would result in an O&M expense of $70m in year 2, and again in year 3, 4, …n.

Even if recurrent costs were only 10% of capital, and they were not lower than this, O&M costs would, by year 10, be equal to the initial capital investment. For hospitals and schools, this would happen in less than two!

So, the argument that capital was declining as a proportion of GDP was more accurately to be stated as the proportion of recurrent costs was increasing! Moreover, if we were to get full value from our capital, these O&M costs were essential.

At my first presentation to the Infrastructure Forum in Canberra in 1988, where the AFCC lobbied the government for more capital funds, I spoke on 'Priority Setting: The Rules of the Game', arguing that we needed to ensure we achieved win-win outcomes and did not build infrastructure that was not needed.

The AFCC was not pleased, and spoke to the CSIRO (the session organisers) to request I not be invited again.

The CSIRO abided by these instructions and did not invite me again. But it did invite the National Centre for Research Board — Facilities Management (NCRB-FM) sub-committee, an association of university facility and public works managers, of which both the CSIRO and I were members. That committee then invited me to speak on its behalf! I used this second appearance to explain this relationship between capital, essential O&M, and GDP.

The AFCC gained some support from a federal government report by Professor John Langmore, who argued that increased infrastructure led to greater productivity. However, the report did not support this conclusion.

John Langmore subsequently became Secretary of the Caucus Economics Committee and continued to promote the infrastructure/productivity link. To be fair to Langmore, this argument was heavily supported at the time in both the USA and the UK, as well as here by the AFCC, but in all places, it was led by construction contractors.

So, while our small but quickly growing group of enthusiastic asset managers had a sound narrative, we didn't have it all our own way. We were outnumbered and outfunded. The fact that, despite this, we continued to grow and attract the interest of audit commissions and governments is evidence that we did indeed have a sound argument. And we continued to promote it.

CHAPTER 18

WHY THIS STORY — AND WHERE TO NOW?

And so we come to the end of the first ten years and our last question.

This book has had a long gestation period. I first started thinking about it in 2010 when I needed to curtail my advisory practice to care for my husband, whose health had sorely deteriorated. At that time, I created the 'Asset Management History Project Forum' on LinkedIn, where I would ask questions of experienced asset managers and we would dialogue. It kept me connected while I could no longer travel.

Then a thoughtful reader, Clare Kirkland, Deputy Minister for Economic Development, Saskatchewan, Canada, challenged me with this question that it is now time to answer:

Q 10: WHAT KIND OF STORY ARE YOU INTENDING TO TELL?

He elaborated: Is it the story of valiant individuals? Well-rooted transformation? Progress limited by imperfect public policy and lack of long-term optimisation?

His question made me ask myself another: 'Why do I care so much, and why should anyone else, including you?' I spent the next three hours considering his question and, as a result, the answer I sent him was very much longer than his question.

I told him that my original reason for wanting to document the path that asset management had taken was purely selfish. I wanted to understand it better myself.

After all, in the early 1980s, books published in the USA described problems created by failing to maintain infrastructure, such as *America in Ruins: The Decaying Infrastructure* (1981) by Choate & Walker, outlining the problem, and *Crumbling Academe* (1984) by Harvey Kaiser, who provided information on how to fund required maintenance for universities and developed some quite innovative programs. Yet neither the USA Government nor the private sector acted. Then, in 1988, the USA publication *Fragile Foundations* created shockwaves for a time by detailing how many billions were needed by way of renewal, upgrade, and expansion. Still, no one in the USA acted.

Meanwhile, a series of eight smaller but well-focused studies on asset renewal for the South Australian Parliament's PAC, carried out over 1985–87, resulted in Australia adopting both improved asset accounting and asset management over a decade before the same things happened in most other places, and almost two decades before they were adopted in the USA. Why did Australian governments, from local to federal, take up the challenge when the far richer USA did not?

There were other puzzles. For example, why did local government in Australia, the least well-funded of the levels of government, take up the challenge considerably in advance of the better-funded federal and state levels?

There are differences in take-up between utilities, manufacturing, and retail, and, of course, in different regions of the world. What caused some to be ahead of the curve and others to lag?

Why is it that in some places, such as the UK, the asset management charge was led at the national level by finance through the Chartered Institute of Public Finance and Accounting (CIPFA) and surveyors, through the Royal Institute of Chartered Surveyors (RICS), while in others, such as Australia, the first to get really interested were local government engineers? Or, that in some areas, the move was bottom-up by practitioners, whilst, in others, it was top-down by policymakers? Which approach has seen the most success? And are these groups gradually moving closer together or further apart?

I told my questioner that as I travelled across Australia and overseas, I discovered interesting techniques being used well by one jurisdiction, yet almost completely unknown by others. Why?

And, sadly, I would see agencies that I had rated in the lead some fifteen to twenty years earlier fall back and need to rediscover what they once knew. Again, why?

For twenty years, I was very closely involved with just about every development in public sector asset management in Australia and many in New Zealand, including much of the policymaking. Now, as an interested observer and chronicler, I told him I wanted to see if I could find answers to these questions.

What kind of story is it?

I told the minister that the story I wanted to tell was not a story of 'valiant individuals', although we would encounter many of them. Nor would I describe what I had to say as a description of 'well-rooted transformation'. In many cases, luck took more of a hand. Well, was it 'progress limited by imperfect public policy and lack of long-term optimisation?'

This, sadly, is too commonly used as an excuse today, but to accept it removes responsibility for future progress from asset managers and casts them into the role of victim, and victimhood is a very weak base from which to move forward.

Thus, my story is rather a story of ideas, of community commitment, and of the search for answers to questions. It is the story of setbacks, yes, but also of forward movement. In essence, it is a story of setting a direction and then looking for opportunities.

I then explained why I thought it necessary for asset managers and others to know this story. I said that today, the major danger is 'mindless compliance' and the related desire to put short-term success ahead of longer-term improvement. Asset managers will typically accuse politicians of this, but we can equally be at fault. Whenever we seek to have our asset management processes mandated so that funding is automatic and we no longer need to justify our actions, we are in danger of losing the very ability to justify. When we settle down to just following routine, we lose the ability to question and, thus, any justification for existing! We also lose the fun of moving forward.

If the story of asset management is to continue, we need to continuously review what we are doing and ask what needs to be done and why. Then we need to be constantly aware of the opportunities that present themselves. It is my hope that this story will encourage such endeavour.

I write for the asset manager who has been in the field for a long time and, like me, seeks to be able to see his/her own experience in a wider context to perhaps make more sense of it; and I am writing for the new asset managers, who can see how far the discipline has come already, and, maybe how much further it has yet to go. I would also like to think that I am writing for the policymakers who can either make or break asset management; but realistically, I see the route through to policymakers as being mostly through better-informed asset managers who take their community responsibility seriously.

I think of the first ten years of asset management (1984 to 1993) as a succession of questions, the answers to which generated yet more questions. Here we have explored the first ten.

So, in a sense, my Canadian interrogator was right. It is a story of valiant individuals — a great many of them. These first ten years are perhaps the story of the asset managers as hero, for they were challenging the status quo, fighting contrary mindsets, and doing so with limited tools and data, but with plenty of enthusiasm, imagination and commitment. As each country has taken up this quest, I have seen the same level of enthusiasm in the initial years.

Here I hope to have answered some questions, but there are more yet to be answered and, indeed, more to be asked!

CHAPTER 19

REACTIONS: OR, 'THE WAY WE SEE THE WORLD DEPENDS ON THE WORLD WE SEE'

A confession

Well, time for me to confess.

I am not, and never have been, an asset manager. You have probably figured this out already!

I am, instead, an asset management strategist. My expertise lies in looking at what asset management can do and what it is doing. While I have never had hands-on responsibility for managing any asset, I have worked with and exchanged ideas with many hundreds who have, across all asset classes, from the humble municipal public toilet to nuclear power stations. I have also had extensive dealings with those who specialise in providing information, equipment, software, and financial advice to asset managers, those who account for, audit, or regulate asset management, and those in government who decide policies that impact asset management. That is what a strategist does.

My interest has been with infrastructure — those asset systems that we can keep operational as long as we want by renewing elements as they wear out, so that the whole system continues to operate. These assets tend not to fail completely, but gradually degrade, so our management decisions are also affected by the level of service we feel we can live with, which brings in social and political issues. In the earlier chapters of this book, I have tended to concentrate on infrastructure assets, and state-owned infrastructure at that, because that is what I have built my understanding of asset management on.

But not all asset managers have infrastructure assets. And now, as we move on to the views of other asset managers, the ideas, arguments, and assumptions will inevitably reflect more non-infrastructure assets.

The world we see

It is only natural that one's views on asset management will be strongly influenced by the type of assets one has to manage. Let me illustrate with just two broad groups: engineering and networks. How might asset managers in each of these groups see the world of asset management?

Take engineering assets, such as power generation, manufacturing, military, and large and complex water-treatment and sewerage-treatment facilities. The world that managers of engineering assets would probably see is one predominantly characterised by:

- plant and machinery assets: mechanical and electrical components with relatively short lifespans, say less than ten, and seldom more than thirty, years

- a range of intervention options that can be adopted at any one time, and where the decision depends on careful data analysis and assessment
- high criticality, where considerable analytical data are available
- each asset generally having just a few technically trained operators/ maintainers who are responsible for just that asset or component, or a cluster of very similar assets
- some specialist outsourcing, but much of the work done in-house or with private partners who work on site alongside in-house staff in close relationships.

Such asset managers will be the most likely to see asset management as a matter of optimisation; they will often use terms such as 'systems engineering' to describe what they do. The focus of their interest is to manage cost, risk, and reliability. Decisions are based on improvements to the bottom line. These asset managers realise that if you can't prove something is worth doing, it probably won't get done. They are the most likely to say, 'If you can't measure it, you can't manage it'.

In sum, they will generally feel they have a fair amount of control over their world.

Now consider network assets such as pipes, wires, roads, power distribution, water distribution, sewerage collection, local government roads, state and federal highways, and stormwater drainage systems. The world that asset managers in this group would probably see is one predominantly characterised by:

- passive civil structures with long lifespans (around thirty to a hundred years or more)
- relatively limited intervention options, particularly for buried assets
- low criticality — the service will generally slowly degrade rather than dramatically stop
- measurement generally by sample and extrapolation, and information relatively scarce — because of the great extent of these assets (and, for buried assets, difficulty of access)

- simpler skills required for operators and maintainers — they will generally be responsible for a wide scope of very similar assets across a geographical area
- frequent outsourcing of maintenance and especially data collection — generally, not much high individual asset management commitment to a particular asset
- no clear financial bottom line. Instead, because such assets can be kept going as long as decision-makers wish, by dint of component renewal or changed standards of service, it is never particularly clear when action is needed or what action is optimal. Decisions are not determined by some objective factor, such as profit, but by subjective social and political factors.

The managers of network assets are thus more likely to see asset management as asset preservation rather than optimisation because there is no ready bottom line of profitability that enables them to determine the optimum level of intervention.

They are more likely to feel that decision-makers (those who determine the budget) fail to appreciate the importance of their assets. Their long-run modelling indicates the importance of today's maintenance and management to overall long-run costs but often fails to capture the commitment of decision-makers in the moment.

They would like to make long-run decisions that would shape the budget, but they probably find themselves making short-run decisions on the best way to allocate the budget they have been given. So, although their assets are the longest living of any of the groups, their actual work may be far more short-term.

In sum, these managers may not feel as much in control as our first group and are more likely to believe they are underfunded. They are also more likely to feel that the route to success is not so much better analysis as achieving more political clout within their organisation or with the community. And in this, they are not far wrong.

There is another category of assets (public buildings or facilities) that has similar characteristics to networks, and where intervention may be socially or politically determined, as well as influenced by economic considerations.

Because they need a similar management style, I include both when I speak of infrastructure — although I am aware that in North America, infrastructure is usually confined to networks, while buildings are considered separately. But both are managed by renewing worn elements to keep them operational as long as desired. True, facilities are more affected by aesthetics and often have an overall shorter life range, but within this, their management is largely the same.

So, as we move onto the next chapter and future volumes, and the stories told by different asset managers, be aware that their reactions will be conditioned by the kind of assets they dealt with, as will yours.

CHAPTER 20

MOVING ON — THEIR STORIES

When we look back, we realise that when we are thrown into a new situation, especially if it is a critical one; or when there is little guidance and we have to sort it out for ourselves; or when we get highly frustrated and are about to quit — these are the moments that a breakthrough often occurs, and we learn something. And while it may not be fun at the time, it can make for the best of stories as we can see from the following.

Our three storytellers, Roger Byrne, James (Jim) Kennedy, and Peter Kohler, are all Asset Management Council MESA medal winners, indicating that they have been awarded for a lifetime of excellence in asset management. Despite decades of service, they are all still actively engaged in AM today.

Our first is an origin story from 1965 as told by Roger Byrne, whom we met earlier in this volume. In 2010, I asked many asset managers to tell me how they started in AM, and this was Roger's story.

Roger's Story — Understanding the not-easily-seen

Roger was instrumental in raising awareness of asset management in Australia and overseas, and he created the forerunner to today's IIMM.

His early experience was with underground assets and civil infrastructure. Roger wrote this for me in 2010 when I asked how people got started in asset management:

> 'Upon graduation in 1965 as a civil engineer, I sought gainful employment. I loved structures and hoped to become a bridge designer. However, the only job I was able to get was as an assistant design engineer with the Commonwealth Department of Works in their Water and Sewerage Division in Melbourne.
>
> One of the first jobs I was given (in 1966) was to investigate why the screens at the sewerage treatment plant (STP) appeared to be blocked by a wood fibre. I eventually traced the source of the wood fibre to the fact that the formwork had been left in all manholes in the sewer system during WW1, and it was disintegrating and passing down the sewer to the STP. Poor contract administration and asset handover, as well as poor operations and maintenance, had allowed this problem to exist for over 50 years.
>
> The result of this revelation was to get a job to plot up all the underground services in the Puckapunyal Army Camp. It had been mainly built in two critical stages during the First and Second World Wars, and few designs and no 'as constructed plans' existed. Aerial photos showed us that many buildings, not shown on plans, existed and many shown did not.
>
> As the topographic and surface infrastructure plans were updated, it was my job to construct the utility services plans (now known as layers in geographic information system (GIS) terms) for the water (potable and irrigation), sewer, drainage, electricity and gas systems across the whole base.
>
> Little did I realise that it was in preparation for the upgrade of the camp for the conscription program for the Vietnam War, for which I would be eligible.

What I learnt was that we knew little about the infrastructure. The existing plans often showed the size and material of the service, but close inspection showed that one, two or all were likely to be wrong. I even had several water plans that turned out to be underground electricity cables.'

Roger then set up a program to record asset details, first on cards and plans and then on the WANG Symphony system (forerunner of Lotus Notes, now mostly replaced by Excel): age, condition, performance, and even current replacement cost (his first wife was an accountant!). From this information, he was able to establish a list of those assets that needed capacity augmentation, those that needed rehabilitation or replacement, and those that needed better-planned maintenance.

His work with putting the data to use showed him that, 'If you apply good life-cycle cost logic using the best data you have available, you will reach a high-quality or high-confidence decision. Don't wait for perfect data; you may never get it, or you may never be able to afford to get it.'

He then went on to work with GHD (Gutteridge, Haskins and Davies), becoming one the most well-known names in asset management in Australia for his passion and his focus on continuous improvement in knowledge and practice.

Other origin stories are available on the Talking Infrastructure website at www.talkinginfrastructure.com/tams.

* * *

Jim's Stories

Our second storyteller is James (Jim) Kennedy, who was responsible for creating The Asset Management Council (AMC) in 2001, out of the Maintenance Engineering Society Australia. Jim's early experience was with the maintenance of military aircraft, followed by the transfer of this technology to the Melbourne and Sydney metro rail systems in the early 1990s. His first story is drawn from military aircraft.

Story 1. The RAAF Analytical Maintenance Philosophy

Jim recounts that in the early 1970s, the Royal Australian Air Force (RAAF) had an evolving view that their maintenance programs, intended to protect the safety and availability of their very expensive and limited numbers of air assets, were not fit for purpose. The plans had no logical process for determining task content or when that content should be implemented.

This view was driven home when, in the mid-1970s, the 24 F-III aircraft purchased in the 1960s were consuming some 50% of the entire RAAF O&M budget. It was clear: 'We could afford to buy it, but we could not afford to own it.'

In 1976, Jim and another RAAF officer travelled to all the major Western military units responsible for establishing maintenance policies and practices, and they discovered that none of the militaries around the world knew how to balance cost, risk, and performance when defining their largest single expenditure: maintenance.

They also did not know how to determine when to do that maintenance in any defensible way. Maintenance was subjective by 'experienced persons', not facts and risk.

The outcome of this discovery was the RAAF Analytical Maintenance Philosophy, the application of which, between 1980 and 1983, is credited with reducing the RAAF's maintenance costs by some 30 to 50%. The real figure will never be known. Jim said, 'This gave me a whole new view of why we did maintenance and how to determine it. It also provided a key skill that would keep me employed for the next 40 years.'

Story 2. Language is 'fluffy'

Jim continued to think about this problem and, in group discussions with my three storytellers, he said that the difficulty in recognising and dealing with ongoing costs was caused by using language rather than maths. He said language was 'fluffy' — and it is! It is hard to get agreement when using only words, as no one is quite sure of how words may be interpreted by others, and we are often not entirely sure about them ourselves.

The group agreed that everybody knows what the maintenance task is. It is to manage a particular failure mode, but the real question is, 'How often?' Given the prevalence of 'human error', where extra damage can be caused during physical interventions, this is an important question.

Jim held that the solution was getting agreement, instead, on the numbers, and he suggested that the way forward was to identify the essential parameters — likely economic life, replacement or renewal cost, annual cost, and the likelihood of failure if action is not taken — and then establish a consensus on these parameters.

This approach not only works with engineers and maintenance professionals but is also very effective in generating understanding and getting councillors on board with the issue of infrastructure renewal, as Jeff Roorda and I had discovered when we had applied it in our approach to local government.

Story 3. A defensible maintenance budget

Later in that conversation with my three practitioners, Jim told a story that was much appreciated by all.

He had won a contract in 2011 to write a business model to put asset management into Maritime for the ongoing support, post-acquisition, of the RAN's largest-ever warships.

After three days in Canberra, and frustrated because he could not get in to talk with any of the key stakeholders, he took himself off to the greenroom where the defence staff had their coffee.

In one corner, a large group was huddled around a big plasma screen TV. He thought they were probably watching the cricket. But no, it was a Senate Estimates Committee Hearing, and they were utterly absorbed in watching their budget proposal being picked apart, really picked apart, by politician Barnaby Joyce. Epiphany!

This is wrong, Jim thought. Nobody should be sent into an estimates committee unless they have the means to defend every cent they have asked for. In this case, little could be readily defended.

So, he went back to his desk and wrote down eight dot points covering what a 'defensible budget' should include, and that became the value proposition of the whole program to create an asset management capability for Australia's largest-ever warships.

You can see those eight dot points and Jim's ideas on a defensible budget, which he now teaches in his training courses, on the Talking Infrastructure website at www.talkinginfrastructure.com/tams.

* * *

Our third storyteller is Peter Kohler, with the most exciting story of them all.

Peter Kohler was perhaps the major contributor to the first edition of ISO 55000. Like Jim, Peter also started his asset management career from a military base of maintenance, but whereas Jim was managing many, very similar, aircraft, Peter's portfolio consisted of military ships, each very expensive but each very different.

Peter's story — Preparing for the Gulf War

Some of us have had the good fortune to learn our asset management gradually, but Peter was thrown in at the deep end. Here is his story:

> 'It was August 1990 and the government had committed to sending three ships to take part in the Gulf War. I was, at the time, Commander of Fleet Maintenance for the Navy. My initial task was to identify and understand the engineering/logistical support available to the Royal Australian Navy (RAN) in the Gulf. Then, with others, we developed

and implemented the foundations for RAN support in the Gulf and so, again with others, to identify which three ships were to go.

This meant identifying the needed ship system configuration, managing the needed changes to the ships and getting the right support in place for the ships in both Australia and the Gulf, including development of contingency plans. For example, how should the RAN respond to any battle damage if that occurs? How will the RAN deliver medical aid to its sailors, if needed?

We needed to identify gaps in RAN leadership and culture and gaps in RAN technical knowledge and competency. This required us to learn from around the world about how to identify and deliver needed support away from Australia, and make subsequent changes (both organisational and technological) to the RAN/Australian Defence Force (ADF).

This was when I realised how little I knew. For example:

- Technological — How do we change the existing maintenance plans to assure that the ships are 'fit for purpose' for action in the Gulf?
- Leadership & Culture — I did not know enough about the value of a 'supportive RAN leadership style and RAN culture' — that is, working as a team. (It was clear we didn't, and we weren't!)
- Integration — I did not know how to bring all this together (but I realised that we/RAN needed to!)

Clearly, we needed clarity about the purpose of the RAN and then what each RAN ship now must do. We then had to get the RAN working together as a team, and to focus on leadership and developing a culture of trust. Do we need to have engineers, supply people, operators, financial people as separate disciplines? Is that a good thing?

We needed to learn available good practice and develop good practice guides.

The RAN organisational structure appeared not fit for purpose. Issues included lack of accountability for outcomes (these were not even documented), the role of engineering, the role of financial practices, the role of integrated logistics support (ILS), etc.

Even if we need to change, can we technically and managerially and culturally do all this? (The conduct of the HMAS Tobruk trial, the use of Standards/Process in the RAN, for example by linking RAN/ship outcomes to maintenance plans/tasks and the available budget, changing our culture.)

Finally, what did we learn about asset management?

Asset management is effective when it is supported by an organisation that is collectively focused on delivering ships that work, is driven by competent and trained people who value working as a team, and has a culture to support that ideal. As a result, an AM system includes:

- a clear focus on what it is that needs to be done
- enabling processes and software/data
- a supportive organisational structure, leadership style and workplace culture.

The value of asset management is twofold. It:

- identifies what needs to be achieved, and
- develops the people, the culture, the processes and the data (that is — develops the supportive AM system) that delivers the requisite level of assurance that what needs to be done will be done!

The term asset management did not come into vogue until sometime later. The military equivalent is Systems Engineering + ILS + Continual Improvement + Leadership and Culture.'

The end of the Gulf War, however, was not the end of the story.

Peter says that after the Gulf War had ended and their three ships and crews had returned intact, the senior officers looked at each other and said, 'We were lucky!'

In the planning time they had before the war, they had been able to define what operational configuration they needed, but they weren't able to find who would be able to tell them whether their ships met that configuration.

Afterwards, when the ships and their crews returned safe and intact, the questions were then: 'What do we have to do to be better equipped next time?' and 'Wouldn't it be nice if we could describe what the output of each of our warships was in a way that we could all understand?'

Peter also told us that, during the Gulf War, what was reliable for the RAN was not what one would expect.

After many months of being on station in the Gulf, the selected warships were not reporting many system failures or requiring significant spares on the ship or sited locally. The ship was accused of misreporting.

However, what had not been realised when planning the deployment was that in this new operational tempo, the ships' systems were never turned off; they operated 24/7. The systems were not failing when used continuously in the same way they did on short-term trips, with systems powered down in between. There was no 'luck' involved. It was a lack of understanding of the drivers for the reliable performance of their assets.

All asset managers can expect to find themselves in a stressful situation at some time, particularly with natural disasters (fire, flood, and pandemics) on the rise. They will not, of course, have the same budget to deploy as the RAN did in this case, which makes it even more important that they know what their assets need to do, and are able to do, and what must happen if the ability does not match the need.

Jim had defined a function of asset management as being the ability to defend every dollar of the budget. But another definition might be knowing what to do when the budget does not match the defined need.

* * *

Common agreement

Although their backgrounds were different, the three storytellers above all agreed on the basics — operations and maintenance over the lifetime of long-living assets swamp the original capital costs, yet that is not well prepared for. They also agreed that each of their current accounting systems told them what they had done and how much it cost, but did not help them look ahead and manage, which is what asset managers need to do. Their accounting systems were designed to report externally, not manage internally. They used financial management, not management accounting.

In 1993, I presented a paper to the National Accountants in Government Conference in Hobart, where I outlined an accounting procedure, 'condition-based depreciation', based on asset management plans that took maintenance into account when calculating depreciation. It integrated management accounting and asset management and was well-received by the audience. Indeed, it was credited with being the paper 'most likely to improve public sector accounting' and was subsequently published.

Unfortunately, in the thirty years that have passed, the opportunity to do this has now disappeared. But the need has not. The original papers are still available on the Talking Infrastructure website at www.talkinginfrastructure. com/tams, and this is an issue that will be picked up in Volume 2.

All three of our leading practitioners in this chapter have something in common, beyond ongoing commitment to asset management, and that is, having discovered a problem, they set about finding a solution to it, and found it to be a never-ending process. They, as did I, found that all solutions suggest yet extra questions. They have all enthusiastically shared their experience with others, through active training, mentoring, and conference presentations. Peter has gone further. Having learnt the importance of trust and leadership from his Gulf War experience, he teamed up with John Hardwick and other leaders at the Living Asset Management Think Tank (Martin Kerr, Michael Killeen, Joao Ricardo Baruso Lafraia, and Sally Nugent) to write *Living Asset Management Maturity: The Role of Leadership and Culture in Asset Management*, 2020.

* * *

Before I close, I would like to leave you with a story from Michael Bendeli that I recorded ten years ago when I was looking at how people got their start in asset management. Michael is now Investment Executive at Infrared Capital Partners, supporting, amongst other things, battery storage portfolio acquisition essential to the further development of renewables.

For me, Michael's story beautifully captures the excitement of asset management.

Michael's Story — Why I find asset management so exciting

'My involvement and keen interest in asset management began in the second half of 2008. I was a mechanical design engineer finishing up a long and enjoyable stint on the Sydney Desalination Project when I was asked to contribute to a project that we (Sinclair Knight Merz and I) were undertaking to devise the asset management strategy for a major urban water utility's critical infrastructure.

I was initially meant to work on the project for about one month, as my knowledge of their corporate databases would prove useful for one aspect of the project, but once I became involved, I found the asset management field entirely engrossing.

This was a world of complex decision-making, dealing with everything from the physical properties of pipes and soils to the regulatory environment of the utility, to the effectiveness of internal business processes and knowledge management systems. A world that requires you to see the big picture while understanding the intricacies of the minutiae. A world where on any given day, I can be working with operators, maintenance crews, scientists, economists, planners, asset managers or general managers.

I was hooked! I was able to expand my role on the project, and so that original one month turned into a new career direction.

I have worked in asset management ever since and am currently completing a Master of Science degree in Water Services Management at the UNESCO-auspiced IHE Delft, in the Netherlands. This degree focuses on the integration of legal, economic, institutional, organisational and technical considerations for the successful provision of infrastructure services. I am currently undertaking my MSc thesis, which I am using to research the nature and effectiveness of the collaborative environment for sharing and progressing (strategic) asset management within the Australian urban water sector.

The human factor of asset management strongly appeals to me. In the current era where we have available a multitude of software, tools, applications and models (which have their value), the indispensable nature of educated professionals with sharp minds cannot be forgotten. Indeed, I think that is one of the great strengths of the asset management community. It contains many talented individuals who take ownership of the challenges they face (perhaps even relish them) and willingly share their wisdom for the progression of the discipline. It is a community that makes me want to actively participate too.

I truly enjoy the many challenges present in asset management and the debates they spur at all different levels: qualitative versus quantitative analysis; prescriptive standards versus supportive guidelines; structural reform of utilities or the encouragement of voluntary alliances; maintenance or renewal; compliance versus innovation.

I have come into the industry at a very interesting time and have been particularly fortunate to have had the guidance and encouragement of a very talented senior practitioner within my firm, as well as the support of my organisation. I can wholeheartedly endorse the value of mentorship in the development of a younger engineer.

If I sound overly excited by asset management, it is because I find working in the field deeply satisfying. I value the fact that the work I do contributes to the sustainable provision of essential services and that, thanks to strategic asset management, decisions influencing hundreds of millions of dollars of (often public) spending can be made prudently.

I look forward to the challenges ahead!'

And so do I!

REFERENCES

The following publications have been mentioned in this book, and may be downloaded from the Talking Infrastructure website at: https://talkinginfrastructure.com/the-asset-management-story/

Chapter 2
PAC Report Water Asset Renewal

Chapter 5
PAC Report 44 Housing Asset Replacement

Chapter 6
PAC Report 53

Chapter 9
The Otis Elevator Story
Asset Management for Quality that Lasts 2006
Asset Management for Quality that Lasts 2017

Chapter 11
If the answer is 2%, what's the question?
Priority Setting, the rules of the game, for the Infrastructure Forum, Canberra
Priority Setting, the rules of the game, for the Local Government Association, Hobart

Chapter 15
The source of value, and the fragrance-free soap

Chapter 20
Jim Kennedy's 8 dot points for a defensible budget

www.ingramcontent.com/pod-product-compliance
Lightning Source LLC
Chambersburg PA
CBHW031848200326
41597CB00012B/322